SECRET BRITAIN

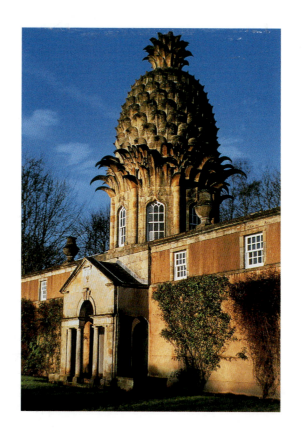

SECRET BRITAIN

Tom Quinn
Photography by Chris Coe

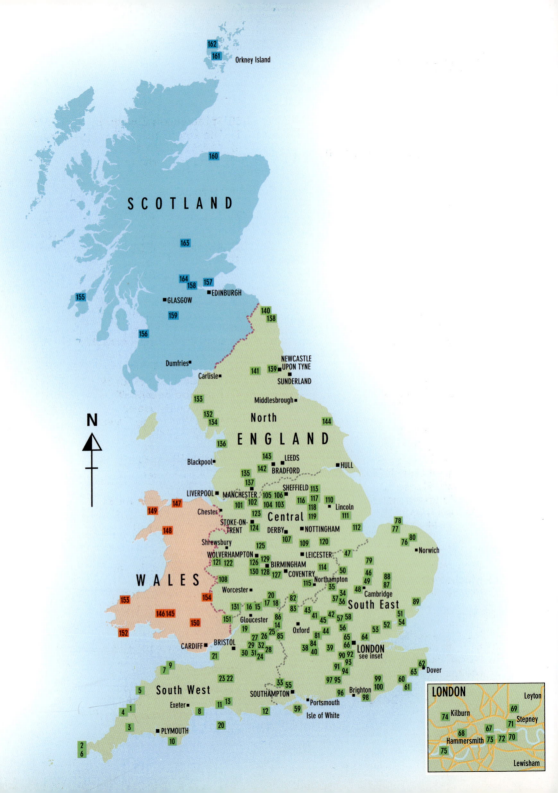

Contents

Introduction 8

ENGLAND – South West 10

CORNWALL 12
1   Tintagel 12
2   Botallack to Penberth 13
3   Lanhydrock 14
4   St Enodoc Church 15
5   Morwenstow 16
6   Porthcurno Beach 17

DEVON 18
7   Arlington Court 18
8   Sidmouth to Branscombe 20
9   Heddon Valley to Woody Bay 21
10 Buckland Abbey 22

DORSET 23
11 Golden Cap 23
12 Studland Beach 24
13 Eggardon Hill 26

GLOUCESTERSHIRE 27
14 Kelmscott 27
15 Cleeve Hill 28
16 Deerhurst Church 29
17 Stanway House 30
18 Hicks' Almshouses 31
19 Owlpen Manor 32
20 Dover's Hill 33

SOMERSET
21 Brean Down 34
22 Muchelney Abbey 36
23 Burrow Mump 37

WILTSHIRE 38
24 Caen Hill Locks 38
25 St John the Baptist Church 39
26 North Meadow 40
27 Malmesbury Abbey 41
28 Silbury Hill 42
29 Maud Heath's Causeway 44

30 St Laurence's Church 45
31 The Peto Garden 46
32 Cherhill Down 48
33 Pepperbox Hill 49

ENGLAND – South East 50

BEDFORDSHIRE 52
34 The Swiss Garden 52
35 Bromham Mill 53
36 Wrest Park 54
37 Flitton Church 55

BERKSHIRE 56
38 St Mary's Church 56
39 Ankerwycke Yew 57
40 Finchampstead Ridges 58

BUCKINGHAMSHIRE 59
41 Waddesdon Manor 59
42 Ivinghoe Beacon 60
43 Claydon House 62
44 West Wycombe Caves 63
45 Coombe Hill 64

CAMBRIDGESHIRE 66
46 Wicken Fen 66
47 Flag Fen 67
48 Wimpole Hall Farm 68
49 Anglesey Abbey 69
50 Little Gidding 70

ESSEX 71
51 Layer Marney Tower 71
52 Thrift Wood 72
53 St Andrew's Church 74
54 St Peter on the Wall 75

HAMPSHIRE 76
55 Mottisfont Abbey 76

HERTFORDSHIRE
56 Gardens of the Rose 77
57 The Fighting Cocks 78
58 Welwyn Roman Baths 79

ISLE OF WIGHT 80
59 Bembridge and Culver Downs 80

KENT 81
60 St Augustine's Church 81
61 Derek Jarman's Garden 82
62 The Grand Shaft 83
63 St Leonard's Church 84

LONDON 85
64 Eastbury Manor House 85
65 Boston Manor House 86
66 The Dove 88
67 Trafalgar Square Lock-up 89
68 Linley Sambourne House 90
69 Geffrye Museum 92
70 Catherine of Aragon's House 93
71 Denis Severs' House 94
72 The George Inn 96
73 Berry Bros & Rudd and Lock & Co. 97
74 Kensal Green Cemetery 98
75 London Wetland Centre 99

NORFOLK 100
76 St Peter and St Paul 100
77 Little Walsingham 101
78 Blakeney Point 102
79 Welney Wildfowl Reserve 103
80 Blickling Hall 104

OXFORDSHIRE 105
81 Stonor Park 105
82 Swalcliffe Barn 106
83 Great Tew 108
84 Mapledurham 109
85 Wayland's Smithy 110
86 St Oswald's Church 111

SUFFOLK 112
87 Ickworth House 112
88 The Nutshell 114
89 Tattingstone Wonder 115

SURREY 116
90 Chatley Heath Semaphore Tower 116
91 Holmbury Hill 117
92 Chaldon Church 118
93 Headley Heath 119
94 Leith Hill 120

SUSSEX 121
95 St Botoph's Church 121
96 Cissbury Ring 122
97 Parham House 124
98 Chyngton Farm 125
99 Bateman's 126
100 Jack Fuller's Pyramid 127

ENGLAND – Central 128

CHESHIRE 130
101 Weaver Hall Museum & Workhouse 130
102 Alderley Edge 131

DERBYSHIRE 132
103 Riley's Graves 132
104 Buxton Opera House 133
105 Speedwell Cavern 134
106 Mam Tor 135
107 Calke Abbey 136

HEREFORDSHIRE 138
108 Croft Ambrey and Croft Castle 138

LEICESTERSHIRE 139
109 Loughborough Bell Foundry 139

LINCOLNSHIRE 140
110 The Jew's House 140
111 Tattershall Castle 141
112 Maud Foster Windmill 142
113 Gainsborough Old Hall 144

NORTHAMPTONSHIRE 145
114 Eleanor Cross 145
115 Church of the Holy Sepulchre 146

NOTTINGHAMSHIRE 147
116 Clumber Park 147
117 Mr Straw's House 148
118 Laxton 149
119 Upton Hall Time Museum 150

RUTLAND 151
120 Clipsham Yews 151

SHROPSHIRE 152
121 Long Mynd 152
122 Wenlock Edge 153

STAFFORDSHIRE 154
123 Cheddleton Flint Mill 154
124 Gladstone Pottery Museum 155
125 Cannock Chase 156

WARWICKSHIRE 158
126 Red House Glass Cone 158
127 Packwood House 159

WEST MIDLANDS 160
128 Bournville 160
129 Soho House 161

WORCESTERSHIRE 162
130 Clent Hills 162
131 Brockhampton 163

ENGLAND – North 164

CUMBRIA 166
132 Eskdale Watermill 166
133 The Printing House Museum 167
134 Duddon Valley 168

LANCASHIRE 169
135 Hall-i'-th'-Wood 169
136 Heysham Head 170

MANCHESTER 171
137 Barton Swing Aqueduct 171

NORTHUMBERLAND 172
138 Beadnell Limekilns 172
139 Stephenson's Cottage 173
140 Bamburgh Castle 174
141 Allen Banks 176

YORKSHIRE 177
142 Piece Hall 177
143 Saltaire 178
144 Bridestones Moor 179

WALES 180

CARMARTHENSHIRE 182
145 Aberdeunant 182
146 Aberglasney Gardens 183

CONWY 184
147 Conwy 184

GWYNEDD 185
148 Portmeirion 185

ISLE OF ANGLESEY 186
149 Newborough Beach 186

MERTHYR TYDFIL 187
150 Joseph Parry's Cottage 187

MONMOUTHSHIRE 188
151 The Kymin 188

PEMBROKESHIRE 189
152 St Govan's Chapel 189
153 Dinas Island 190

POWYS 192
154 The Begwyns 192

SCOTLAND 194

ARGYLL & BUTE 196
155 Bowmore Distillery 196

AYRSHIRE 197
156 Crossraguel Abbey 197

FIFE 198
157 Inchcolm Island 198
158 Culross 200

LANARKSHIRE 201
159 New Lanark 201

MORAY 202
160 Tugnet Ice House 202

ORKNEY 203
161 Dounby Click Mill 203
162 Maeshowe Tomb 204

PERTH & KINROSS 206
163 Wade's Bridge 206

STIRLINGSHIRE 207
164 Dunmore Pineapple

Picture credits 208

Introduction

When you look at Britain on a map of the world, it soon becomes apparent that the country is a modestly proportioned offshore island. Three distinct countries: England, Scotland and Wales make up Britain. And, for all its apparent small size the island has an extraordinary variety of landscapes: from the wild hills and fells of Scotland, the Lake District and Northumberland, to the flat plains and ancient villages of East Anglia; and the tiny fishing villages and hidden beaches of Cornwall and Devon to the quiet downs and meadows of Kent and Sussex. Then there are rocky, wildlife-rich coastlines, mudflats and estuaries, lowland meadows and ancient farms, gin-clear chalk streams and broad, rain-fed rivers.

The rich diversity of this landscape is matched – if not exceeded – by the extraordinary architectural wealth of Britain's villages and towns. There is hardly a place in the entire country that does not contain something of interest: ancient abbeys, early almshouses and timber-framed cottages, magnificent country houses and castles, tiny churches and fortified manor houses.

Of course, much of England, Scotland and Wales is already well known. Visitors from both home and abroad discovered long ago the delights of Bath and Stonehenge, Burghley House and Westminster Abbey – and, indeed, of many less famous places – but the huge amount that remains to be explored is the main justification for this book. It is all too easy to miss the gems that hide behind the more obvious landmarks: places such as the Jew's House in Lincoln, which is the oldest domestic building in Britain; the historic semaphore tower at Chatley Heath in Surrey; or the country's last remaining wooden Saxon church, tucked away in the Essex countryside at Greensted.

Away from these wonderful architectural survivals, often in the more remote corners of the countryside, can be found a wealth of stunning landscapes and habitats that are almost too numerous to mention: quiet hilltops, lush, secluded valleys and wide open fens.

This book could have been called 'Forgotten Britain', but the truth is that many of the places described here are not forgotten at all – or at least not entirely. Local people and those 'in the know' have long enjoyed the hidden gems on their doorsteps. No one, I'm sure, would be more delighted than they to know that with the publication of this book the places of which they are so proud will be enjoyed by a wider circle.

An Italianate villa in the Welsh village of Portmeirion.

ENGLAND

South West

WITH ITS LONG sandy beaches, tiny forgotten coves and hidden inland villages, the South West of England is a land apart. Here you can visit Merlin's Cave in Cornwall, as well as the eccentric Lanhydrock House, and the granite church of St Enodoc. In Devon you can visit the ancient Cistercian abbey that was once the home of Sir Francis Drake or, in Somerset, walk the spectacular limestone peninsular of Brean Down. In Wiltshire visit the extraordinary church of St John Inglesham. Wherever you go, you'll find beautiful places to stay from ancient inns to delightful private houses offering bed and breakfast.

Tintagel

CORNWALL

Despite its fame as one of the sites associated with the legendary King Arthur, Tintagel has been neglected in recent years by all except hard-line Arthurians – which is a huge pity because, quite apart from its legendary associations, Tintagel has some of the world's most beautiful coastline, with unrivalled views across the Atlantic. The ruins of the castle date back to the 13th century, long after Arthur is supposed to have departed for Avalon, but they are still magical, either on a bright summer's day or perhaps, more especially, when the autumn mists roll in off the sea.

Then there's the ancient, crooked, 14th-century slate-built manor house, now known as the Old Post Office, which has been beautifully restored by the National Trust. It became the letter-receiving office for this part of Cornwall in 1844 following the introduction of the penny post. It's a gorgeous, picturesque little building, furnished with just the sort of crude, but rather lovely oak country furniture it would have had centuries ago.

If you walk for just half a mile from the ruined castle you reach Tintagel Island and the ruins of what was once thought to be a monastery but is now believed to have been a trading centre at the heart of sophisticated links with the Mediterranean. Archaeologists have found masses of pottery fragments, which have been traced to manufacturing centres in Spain; little has been found, on the other hand, to confirm any of the Arthurian tales.

The ruins of the 13th-century castle.

SECRETS

TINTAGEL VISITOR CENTRE, Bossiney Road, Tintagel, Cornwall, PL34 0AJ ☎ 01840 779084.

While you're there

Visit **MERLIN'S CAVE** at the bottom of the cliffs below the castle. Legend has it that Merlin lived here! Visiting is possible only at low tide.

ST NECTAN'S GLEN is considered one of the most spiritual places in Britain. The breathtaking walk ends with a waterfall.

Secret place to stay

CORNISHMAN INN, Tintagel (cornishmaninn.com). Far better than many bigger and more expensive establishments, this comfortable b&b serves great food and has an enviable reputation.

Botallack to Penberth CORNWALL

This beautiful and historic stretch of coastline deserves to be far better known. It begins a little to the north of St Just at the village of Botallack, which was once an important tin-mining town. The machinery associated with the long-disused Crowns Mine remains clinging precariously to the cliffs below the village, but as the waves eat away at the rocks it is only a matter of time before the remaining structure vanishes into the sea. All along the coast here are similar echoes of the past in the form of old engine houses – the last visible remains of Cornwall's most famous industry. Hidden beneath the cliffs, of course, are untold miles of forgotten and long-closed-up tunnels.

At Penberth Cove small fishing boats are still launched from the secluded beach – this is a glimpse of Cornwall as it might have been a century and more ago. The Penberth Valley is interesting for the remains of tiny meadows, or quillets as they were known locally – delicate flowers like violets were once grown commercially here.

Windswept and battered by gales, this stretch of coastline – taken as a whole – is an extraordinary mix of cliff, cove and headland; and wherever you walk the skies are filled with birds, including fulmar, cormorant, shag, kittiwake and guillemot.

For the archaeology enthusiast, the pattern of fields a little inland is a source of endless wonder, for many of the field patterns here are extremely ancient – certainly pre-Christian and in some places prehistoric.

The remains of the Crowns tin mine.

SECRETS

While you're there

Visit nearby **BALLOWALL BARROW (CARN GLOOSE)**, where there is a Bronze Age tomb to investigate, and the ruins of Maen Castle cliff-top fort near Sennen Cove harbour, which dates back to the Iron Age.

Secret place to stay

THE SHIP INN, Mousehole (shipmousehole.co.uk). Twenty minutes' drive from Botallack, overlooking one of Britain's loveliest harbours.

Lanhydrock

CORNWALL

We fell deeply out of love with all things Victorian during the middle decades of the 20th century, and it has taken more than a century, since the death of Queen Victoria, for us to see more clearly the virtues of the late Victorian period. One of the very best examples of unspoiled high Victorian architecture is Lanhydrock, which lies hidden away in the remote Fowey Valley surrounded by 365ha (900 acres) of ancient parkland.

Parts of the house, most notably the gatehouse and north wing, are 17th century but the rest was rebuilt, with no expense spared, in 1881, after a fire destroyed much of the original structure. Even the central heating is Victorian! The gardens in summer are a delight, with their superb collections of rhododendrons, camellias and magnolias. You could spend days wandering the miles of footpaths that cross the estate, through which the river Fowey runs.

Originally built by Sir Richard Robartes in 1620, the house gradually decayed over the following centuries until the Victorian Lord Robartes returned from London to the house of his ancestors and set about rebuilding. Twenty years after the celebrated architect George Gilbert Scott (famous for renovating medieval churches) rebuilt the house, it burnt down. Richard Coad, a local architect, then rebuilt it, and the house we see today is substantially as he left it. A hidden gem.

SECRETS

LANHYDROCK, Bodmin, Cornwall, PL30 5AD (nationaltrust.org.uk). ☎ 01208 265950. Open: Garden 10.00–18.00. House Tues–Sun Mar–early Nov 11.00–17.30. Check website for latest house and garden opening details. Price: House and garden: adult £11.80, child £5.90, family £29.50,. Garden and grounds: adult £7, child £3.80.

While you're there

Visit TRERICE, Kestle Mill, near Newquay, Cornwall (nationaltrust.org.uk). An unbelievably beautiful and little-known Elizabethan gem of a house.

Secret place to stay

BOSCUNDLE MANOR, Boscundle (boscundlemanor.co.uk). Pretty, privately run hotel in 2ha (5 acres) of grounds. Just 1 mile from Cornwall's famous Eden project.

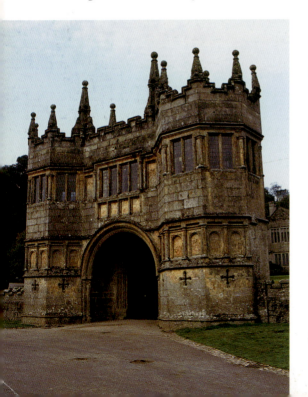

The splendid gatehouse at Lanhydrock.

St Enodoc Church

CORNWALL

St Enodoc Church, below Brea Hill, was, for many years, quite literally buried in the sand, which may explain why it is relatively unknown, even today. It stands above Daymer Bay on a stretch of the Cornish coast that the late Poet Laureate John Betjeman (1906–84) loved above all others. Indeed this is where he is buried. Daymer Bay is a mass of child-friendly rock pools and wide skies – it is also popular with surfers.

The coastal path between St Enodoc and Polzeath is – unlike most of Cornwall's coastal paths – suitable for everyone, from the fittest to those who use wheelchairs. Yet it still offers the sort of fabulous scenery that nowhere else in the world can quite match.

St Enodoc is basically 12th century. When restoration work began in 1912 the sand was so high around the church that it was almost impossible to get in. When the restorers finally cleared a path into the church they found that the pews and other woodwork had turned green with mould. The £600 spent on restoration cleaned the place up, repaired the windows and let the sun shine in once more. The isolation of the church from any village or hamlet is one of the great mysteries about it, and it may be that the church was built on a site of pagan worship, as many early churches were. It was as if those early church builders had to replace every pagan shrine, however inconvenient its location. 'Replacing' quite literally meant putting the Christian edifice on top of the pagan building – the Christians were clearly intent on suppressing the old faiths literally as well as metaphorically.

St Enodoc Church is utterly unspoilt.

SECRETS

While you're there

Nearby **PORT ISAAC** is a picturesque fishing village with narrow winding streets. The remains of a pier dating from the reign of Henry VIII are still visible.

Secret place to stay

ST ENODOC HOTEL, Rock (enodoc-hotel.co.uk). In the heart of Rock, a summertime mecca for sailing and waterskiing, the hotel is set within the most beautiful and dramatic scenery that Cornwall has to offer.

Morwenstow

CORNWALL

Morwenstow is a glorious, easily missed little village just across the border from Devon into Cornwall. For centuries this was a wreckers' village, a place that made much of its living by salvaging ships that foundered in the rough seas off the coast. It has often been said that the law of salvage, which allowed goods to be taken by locals only if all those on board the ship had perished, led to dreadful acts of murder, and no doubt, in desperate times such acts were committed here.

Today, those visitors who stumble across this delightful place come in search of lovely walks along the cliffs to Duckpool, or they explore the coves and bays of this lonely coast.

This is the parish once made famous by the Reverend Stephen Hawker (1803–75), who invented the harvest festival ceremony that most churches and schools now celebrate each year. He was also a poet and an eccentric, who clambered down the most dangerous cliffs to collect the bodies of drowned sailors and make sure they were properly buried.

Hawker had something of the medieval hermit about him, and the tiny hut where he contemplated the world – and, no doubt, eternity – still exists. Parson Hawker wrote 'The Song of the Western Men', the hymn that has become the Cornish national anthem. Its stirring verses begin: 'And shall Trelawney die? Then twenty thousand Cornishmen shall know the reason why.'

The vicarage at Morwenstow has an array of unusual chimneys.

SECRETS

While you're there

Visit the VICARAGE where Hawker commissioned a local builder to make his chimney stacks in the shape of church towers!

Secret place to stay

BELL BUOY COTTAGE, Morwenstow ☎ 0844 847 1115. This 18th-century thatched cottage enjoys its own secluded south-facing garden, and has been tastefully refurbished to retain beams, low ceilings and an inglenook fireplace.

Porthcurno Beach

CORNWALL

Away from the crowds and some 5km (3 miles) south east of Land's End is the wide beautiful beach at Porthcurno. Just above one end of the beach is the improbably situated Minack Open Air Theatre, where you can watch Shakespeare's plays being performed to the sound of the waves on the sands.

You can walk east to Penberth Cove or west to Gwennap Head from here. At Porthcurno itself, there is the remarkable Telegraph Museum. Tunnels were dug here during the Second World War and cables were positioned under the beach and out to sea to the furthest corners of the Empire. This was Cornwall's wartime communications site. The blast-proof doors into the tunnels now house vintage telegraph equipment dating to the 1870s. Check locally for opening times.

View towards the rugged Logan Rock.

SECRETS

While you're there

Visit the National Trust's **PENBERTH COVE**, just to the east along the coast, where open boats can still be seen on the granite slipway.

Secret place to stay

THE OLD SUCCESS INN, Sennon Cove ☎ 01736 871232. A delightful 17th-century fisherman's inn on one of Cornwall's most beautiful bays.

SECRETS

ARLINGTON COURT, near Barnstaple, Devon, EX31 4LP (nationaltrust.org.uk). ☎ 01271 850296. Open: House and Carriage Museum mid Mar–Oct 11.00–15.00. Limited access Feb, Nov, Dec. Price: adult £8.30, child £4.10, family £21, family (1 adult) £13.10. Gardens and Carriage Museum only: adult £6.30, child £3.10.

While you're there

Visit **DUNSTER CASTLE**, Dunster, near Minehead, Somerset (nationaltrust.org.uk). Just short of 40 miles away and a drive through Exmoor National Park, this ancient site was remodelled in Victorian times and is still impressive.

Secret place to stay

YEO DALE, Barnstaple (yeodalehotel.co.uk). A splendid Georgian-fronted house.

Arlington Court

DEVON

The Devon architect Thomas Lee built Arlington in 1822 for Colonel John Chichester, whose family had owned the estate since the middle of the 14th century. But what is most remarkable about this relatively little-known house is that the living rooms are almost exactly as Lee left them more than 150 years ago. Much of the furniture we see today was made specifically for the house by a Barnstaple furniture maker and each piece is still in the place it was made for.

Arlington also gets its special atmosphere from the extraordinary amount of clutter lying around in the house, most of it collected by Miss Rosalie Chichester, who was born in the house in 1865 and lived there until her death in 1949. Miss Chichester – a relative of round-the-world sailor Sir Francis Chichester – collected vast numbers of model sailing ships, pictures of ships, shells, candle snuffers, and much more. She filled the house with caged birds but allowed only the parrots to fly around at will. Rosalie introduced Shetland ponies and Jacob sheep to the grounds, and their descendants can be seen roaming there today. A wonderful collection of horse-drawn carriages is housed in the stable block.

The Regency house of Arlington Court is set in 19th-century gardens.

Sidmouth to Branscombe DEVON

Branscombe retains a number of working historic buildings, such as this forge.

Despite the best efforts of modernizers and town planners, Sidmouth, with its splendid position overlooking Lyme Bay, retains the air of an unspoilt and prosperous Regency seaside town. It is a place of elaborate wrought-iron balconies, flower-filled gardens and stunningly attractive houses.

Landslips blocked the town harbour centuries ago, and now the river Sid slides slowly into the sea over the pebbled beach.

Leaving the town and walking to the east you climb steep cliffs to spectacular views. Look back over Sidmouth for a view as good as you'd get from a helicopter, and then head on to Salcombe Hill, where the views are even better. You should be able to see a mass of white and red that is Dunscombe Cliff. From Salcombe Hill the path drops quickly to Salcombe Mouth and its shingle beach then rises again to reach a plateau before a steep drop takes you to Branscombe Mouth.

SECRETS

While you're there

BRANSCOMBE VILLAGE, which is a short way inland, has the air of a place forgotten by time with its quiet lanes and thatched cottages, truly an area of outstanding natural beauty.

Secret place to stay

BRANSCOMBE HOUSE, Branscombe (branscombehouse.co.uk). Converted and extended from two original cottages, it has traditional decor and antique furnishings.

Heddon Valley to Woody Bay DEVON

If glorious views and walking are for you, the Heddon Valley and Woody Bay offer some of the most unspoilt countryside and coastline you could wish for. Start at the Hunter's Inn in the Heddon Valley and take a path along the river bank. Walk through ancient oaks before reaching cliffs and passing a track that leads to a Roman fort discovered in 1960.

This is beautiful hidden country where you are almost bound to find yourself alone with the woods and the distant seas. When you reach the shingle beach of Heddon's Mouth you are in the centre of an area of outstanding natural beauty. The almost primeval air of the woodlands of the Heddon Valley is filled with birds, butterflies and other wildlife. On the beach is a restored 19th-century limekiln – in

Woody Bay in all its summer glory.

former times lime was burnt in many parts of the country to provide cheap fertilizer.

The Hangman Hills can be reached via nearby Combe Martin. A steep path leads into the heart of this wonderful countryside. Climb Little Hangman (just over 213m/700ft) then continue along the coastal path to Great Hangman (320m/1,050ft), the highest cliff in southern England.

Buckland Abbey

DEVON

This is one of those rare and fabulous English houses that has been many different things in its long life. It began as a Cistercian abbey in the mid-1200s but eventually became the home of one of England's greatest seafarers – Sir Francis Drake. Yet despite Drake's fame the house itself is not nearly as well known as it should be.

In 1539 Henry VIII evicted the monks, took possession of the house and two years later sold it to Sir Richard Grenville, who began the work of converting the monastic buildings. This work was more or less completed by his grandson, also Sir Richard.

SECRETS

BUCKLAND ABBEY, Yelverton, Devon, PL20 6EY (nationaltrust.org.uk). ☎ 01822 853607. Open: mid-Feb–mid-Dec generally 11.00–16.30; restrictions Mar, Nov, Dec; mid-Mar–Oct 10.30–17.30. Price: Abbey, garden and estate: adult £8.05, child £4.05, family £20.20.

While you're there

Visit FINCH FOUNDRY, Sticklepath, Devon ☎ 01837 840046. The last remaining water-powered forge in England.

Secret place to stay

LEWTRENCHARD MANOR HOTEL, Okehampton (lewtrenchard.co.uk). ☎ 01566 783222. Jacobean manor in a hidden valley.

The second Sir Richard inserted three floors into the huge vaulted interior, so he could use the church as a house, but enough space was left for his great hall, which remains remarkably unaltered to this day. The fireplace is dated 1576.

Sir Francis Drake bought the house in 1580 and it remained in his family – two 18th-century Drakes were admirals – until the early 19th century. Drake planned his defeat of the Spanish Armada here, so it is perhaps fitting that the house is now home to the Drake Naval, Folk and West Country Museum. Drake's own drum is still in the house. The abbey's original tithe barn, at 49m (160ft) long, one of the biggest in the country to survive – is just a few yards from the house.

Buckland Abbey's distinctive tower reveals the building's religious origins.

Golden Cap

DORSET

Golden Cap, at 191m (626ft) above sea level, is the highest point on the south coast. All around is evidence of massive cliff erosion. The huge areas of collapsed cliff face, being now inaccessible to human interference, have become a haven for numerous wildlife species: from newts, toads, badgers and slow worms to rare birds of prey, foxes and several species of deer. At the bottom of the cliff is a band of blue lias rock which is rich in fossil remains; and above that lies the golden gravel from which the cap takes its name.

The view from Golden Cap out over these wildlife sanctuaries and across the sea is breathtaking; then, if you head down the western slope of the Cap, you reach the little stream known as St Gabriel's Water. Inland, about a mile along this stream, you'll find the ruins of 13th-century St Gabriel's Church. Where the stream tumbles into the sea there is a shingle beach that is so secluded it was, for centuries, a favourite landing place for smugglers.

Golden Cap is part of a large tract of land owned by the National Trust, and there are more than 29km (18 miles) of footpaths, so it's a place to enjoy at your leisure. Check the tide times carefully though.

The beach at Golden Cap.

SECRETS

While you're there

Pop into nearby LYME REGIS with its wonderful cobb – a stone-walled artificial harbour made famous in the film, *The French Lieutenant's Woman*.

Secret place to stay

BURTON CLIFF HOTEL, Burton Bradstock ☎ 01308 897205. Built in the 1890s, this seaside villa has great views.

Studland Beach

DORSET

Here, at the turn of the 20th century, before British beaches were deserted by tourists for warmer climes overseas, the English well-to-do came to bathe. Among the visitors were Virginia Woolf and her sister, the painter Vanessa Bell. The secluded beach and warm shallow seas have something of the Mediterranean about them, and the sand dunes are an important wildlife habitat.

The beach stretches for 5km (3 miles) from Handfast Point and Old Harry Rocks to South Haven Point, and includes Shell Bay. Behind the beach is an area of sandy heathland which is a designated national nature reserve – it really is fragile and special with many species of bird, plant, insect and reptile including adders, deer, foxes and rare butterflies.

This is actually the extreme eastern end of what was once the Great Dorset Heath – it is a remnant that has survived miraculously amid the development of the Poole conurbation.

SECRETS

While you're there

Visit **DURDLE DOOR**, a remarkable limestone natural archway eroded by the sea.

Secret place to stay

MORTONS HOUSE HOTEL, Corfe Castle (mortonshouse.co.uk). This 16th-century manor house, now an award-winning luxury hotel and restaurant, is located in the picturesque village of Corfe Castle.

Eggardon Hill

DORSET

Windswept and lonely even today, Eggardon must have been an awe-inspiring place when, thousands of years ago, its hill fort was constructed to gaze out over the endless bear- and wolf-filled forest that completely covered the lowlands and valleys. The Iron Age fort – which covers an impressive 16ha (40 acres) – still has its magnificent ramparts and ditches, and almost certainly preserves intact, deep beneath the soil, some splendid archaeological riches, as the site has not been excavated in modern times.

Thomas Hardy called the hill Haggardon in his novel, *The Trumpet Major*, and it is as bleak and beautiful as the author's greatest novels. On a clear day you can see the sea in one direction and Dorset's highest hill – Pilsdon Pen – in the other. The National Trust owns part of the site and allows open access year round.

Eggardon Hill has a wild and desolate beauty.

SECRETS

While you're there

Visit **BEAMINSTER** with its lovely streets of 17th- and 18th-century houses and its excellent museum.

Secret place to stay

GRAY'S FARMHOUSE, Toller Porcorum (farmhousebnb.co.uk). Offers peaceful views of glorious countryside.

Kelmscott

GLOUCESTERSHIRE

Kelmscott Manor is built of local limestone and is a delightful place to visit especially for those who are familiar with the work of Morris.

The fact that Kelmscott Manor House survives in its largely unaltered state is thanks to the great pioneer of the Arts and Crafts movement William Morris (1834–96). In an age when the historical integrity of ancient buildings was largely ignored, Morris cared for Kelmscott in a way that would be admired by modern conservators. Kelmscott is a limestone manor at the edge of the river Thames, and near the town of Lechlade in Oxfordshire. It was built in 1600 and is filled with the furniture and pictures brought here by Morris, his family and friends, including the great Pre-Raphaelite painter Dante Gabriel Rossetti. The house has beautiful fireplaces and carved beams and a well-stocked garden and orchard. Several houses in the village were built in the vernacular style by architect friends of Morris who were part of the Arts and Crafts Movement.

SECRETS

KELMSCOTT MANOR, Kelmscott, Lechlade, Gloucester, GL7 3HJ (kelmscottmanor.co.uk). ☎ 01367 252486. Open: House and garden Apr–Oct Wed & Sat 11.00–17.00. Price: adult £9, child £4.50. Admission is by timed ticket.

While you're there

Just a few miles away is the quaint town of **BURFORD** with its quintessentially English ancient inns, crooked houses and the winding river Windrush – a great place to spend an afternoon shopping.

Secret place to stay

THE LAMB INN, Burford, Oxfordshire (cotswold-inns-hotels.co.uk). ☎ 01993 823155. An early Cotswold-stone building with cosy bars filled with antiques.

Cleeve Hill

GLOUCESTERSHIRE

A 405-ha (1,000-acre) common is topped by Cleeve Hill, which is the highest point in the Cotswolds at 330m (1,080ft) above sea level. From this wild place you can see far off across the Severn Vale and Malvern Hills, the Forest of Dean and, even farther away, the Black Mountains.

Below and behind Cleeve Hill there are three valleys and streams whose heavily wooded slopes are little seen by visitors even on the busiest summer day – somehow they always remain quiet, but they are filled with the sound of birdsong, and badgers, foxes and deer live here undisturbed.

Back on the top of Cleeve Hill the common still preserves the ancient right for 24 local people to graze their animals each summer on the rich limestone grassland – a right that dates back more than 1000 years – and which was reaffirmed in the 1920s. The common and hill represent a landscape that was common prior to the great Enclosure Acts of the late 18th and early 19th centuries. These acts effectively removed what had previously been 'common' land, farmed and grazed by parishioners, to the hands of powerful landowners.

Among the increasingly rare plants that thrive on this largest area of unspoilt grassland in Gloucestershire are small scabious and horseshoe vetch, carline thistle and burnet-saxifrage. Butterflies such as the beautiful dark-green fritillary are seen here; as well as glow-worms and the Roman snail, a creature introduced as a source of food more than 2,000 years ago.

SECRETS

While you're there

Visit the **TOY MUSEUM**, Stow-on-the-Wold (thetoymuseum.co.uk). ☎ 01451 830159. The museum showcases one of the best private collections of toys in the country. Telephone for opening times as these vary considerably.

Secret place to stay

RISING SUN HOTEL, Cheltenham (risingsunhotel-cheltenham.co.uk). Right on top of Cleeve Hill with spectacular views and perfectly situated to explore the local towns and villages.

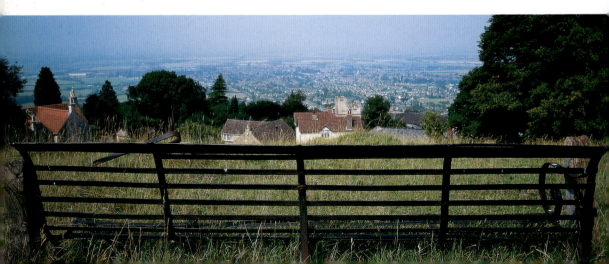

Deerhurst Church

GLOUCESTERSHIRE

Nowhere in the world is quite like the village of Deerhurst – it is rare to have one Saxon building in a village, but Deerhurst, tucked away in a remote corner of Gloucestershire, has two.

The Priory Church of St Mary, with its large, distinctive tower, looks medieval or perhaps Tudor from a distance, but at close view it is quickly apparent from the decorative features that this is a Saxon structure. The first record of this church dates back to 804 – a period still known as the Dark Ages. It is said that kings from this time were buried here.

The tower has distinctive herringbone masonry details as well as curious animal-head carvings. An angel carved high on the wall of the ruins of the apse is one of the earliest recorded in the country. Construction on the original rectangular part of the building is thought to have begun in the late 600s. The polygonal apse is generally agreed to be 9th-century work, along with the chapels, and the porch was added in the 10th century. The font, with its spiral carved decoration is thought to be one of the country's oldest. There are pointed Saxon windows, a small Saxon doorway and stained glass dating from around 1300.

The farmhouse that sits next to the church dates from the same era and was almost certainly part of a series of monastic buildings.

RIGHT: The Church of St Mary in Deerhurst.

LEFT: The sweeping view from Cleeve Hill.

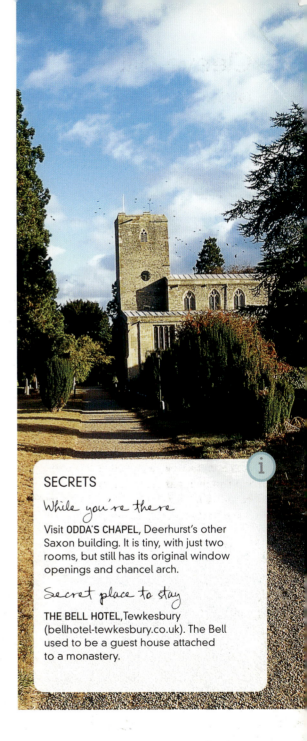

SECRETS

While you're there

Visit **ODDA'S CHAPEL**, Deerhurst's other Saxon building. It is tiny, with just two rooms, but still has its original window openings and chancel arch.

Secret place to stay

THE BELL HOTEL, Tewkesbury (bellhotel-tewkesbury.co.uk). The Bell used to be a guest house attached to a monastery.

Stanway House

GLOUCESTERSHIRE

Stanway House, deep in the heart of the Cotswolds, but away from many obvious tourist centres, is a most remarkable place. Only two families have lived here since the 8th century. The current Lord Niedpath is a direct descendant of the Tracy and Charteris branches of the family. They bought the estate in the late 16th century from the abbots of Tewkesbury, who had owned it since about 800. Most of the buildings we see now were completed by 1680 but work began on them in the 1640s.

The house is built in a wonderful yellow Cotswold stone, with a magnificent gatehouse and great hall. Much of the furniture, which is still used by the family, dates back to when the house was first built. There is a curious sprung chair that was designed for indoor riding on rainy days, and an enormously long refectory table, made from one huge oak plank, which was almost certainly made specially for the house. There is also a unique pair of Chinese Chippendale daybeds made in 1760 and an Elizabethan shuffle board (a board game), also almost certainly original to the house.

Manorial courts were held in the house until 1800, and even today tenants from the village pay their rents each quarter using a specially built circular table. The gatehouse, which is magnificent and was completed in 1630, is positioned at right angles to the house, an odd arrangement that gives it a distinctive, almost eccentric air. The grounds boast the tallest fountain in Britain.

The elegant drawing room in Stanway House.

SECRETS

STANWAY HOUSE, Stanway, Cheltenham, Gloucestershire, GL54 5PQ (stanwayfountain.co.uk/index.html). ☎ 01386 584469. Open: House Jun, Jul & Aug, Tues & Thurs 14.00–17.00. Price: adult £7, child £2, family £15.

While you're there

Visit GREAT BARRINGTON, a lovely quiet village on the river Windrush.

Secret place to stay

THE FOX INN, Great Barrington (foxinnbarrington.com). A delightful, quiet, old-fashioned place right on the river.

Hicks' Almshouses

GLOUCESTERSHIRE

We know that King Harold owned what is now the picture-postcard village and lands of Chipping Campden, and that they were incorporated into the kingdom of Wessex before the Norman Conquest of 1066.

The 'Campden' part of the name means 'valley with fields'; an apt description of the landscape in which it sits. 'Chipping' came to be used by the 1200s to mean a market, which was held in the town. Most visitors to the village simply admire the golden stone of the buildings – but Chipping Campden hides some very special buildings indeed.

By the 14th century the town was remarkably prosperous, its wealth built almost entirely on wool. The Woolstaplers' Hall, an extraordinary survivor in the high street and now a museum, dates back to 1340, when it was thought to be a trading hall. Among the wealthy individuals who became rich on the wool trade was Sir Baptist Hicks who, on his death, wanted to leave something for the good of the poor and of his soul. In 1612 he had a group of almshouses built to home 'six poor men and six poor women', a purpose they still fulfil to this day. Sir Baptist Hicks was one of the richest men in England, but the £1,000 he spent on the almshouses was a staggering sum by the standards of the time.

Almshouses survive in many old English towns to house the deserving poor.

SECRETS

While you're there

Visit the **BLISS TWEED MILL** at Chipping Norton. A working mill until 1980, it was later converted into luxury flats, but is still a magnificent edifice with an unusual chimney that is worth taking the trip to see.

Secret place to stay

OLD NEW INN, Bourton-on-the-Water (www.theoldnewinn.co.uk). A great mix of ancient and modern, with its own tourist attraction – a scaled replica model of the village of Bourton-on-the-Water as it looked in the 1930s.

Owlpen Manor

GLOUCESTERSHIRE

When you look at this house and its setting it is very difficult to understand how our 18th and 19th-century forebears could happily demolish hundreds of similar houses on the premises that they were quaint and old-fashioned – precisely those qualities that we now value so highly.

Owlpen deserves to be better known, for it is the quintessence of Englishness. The Tudor manor house – which began life in 1450 and has been little altered since about 1610 – sits in a quiet wooded valley in one of the few remaining remote areas of the Cotswolds. Owlpen has nothing to do with owls – in Old English the name means the 'land enclosed by Olla', presumably a chieftain. By the 12th century the de Olepenne family was living here. Then in the early 15th century the house and land passed to the Daints, who kept it until the early 20th century. In 1925 the estate was broken up and sold. By sheer good luck the old manor house, which had been empty for almost a century, was bought and carefully repaired by the Arts and Crafts architect Norman Jewson.

Today, Owlpen sits at the centre of a cluster of historic buildings, including a mill dating from 1728 and a group of cottages, some of which are available for rent. The manor house – which houses a collection of Arts and Crafts furniture – still has its Tudor great hall, another great chamber with tapestries dating from 1700 and a beautiful early-Georgian parlour

Owlpen Manor is surrounded by beech woods.

SECRETS

OWLPEN MANOR, near Uley, Gloucester, GL11 (owlpen.com). ☎ 01453 860261. Opening times vary, so check website.

While you're there

Visit medieval **SUDELEY CASTLE** just 13km (8 miles) away (sudeleycastle.co.uk).

Secret place to stay

WHITE HART INN, Winchcombe (whitehartwinchcombe.co.uk). ☎ 01242 602359. Charming 16th-century inn in the heart of an historic town.

Dover's Hill

GLOUCESTERSHIRE

Named after Robert Dover, the 17th-century historian, this natural amphitheatre looks out over the ancient Cotswold town of Chipping Campden and far beyond to Stratford and Warwick. It was in 1612 that Dover resurrected the idea of the Olympic Games and they were held here from 1612 right up until 1851, when they stopped, largely because so many competitors were being injured – hardly surprising when you consider that one of the chief sports was shin kicking!

Today, the broad green acres of this wonderful hilltop are sheep-covered and it is difficult to believe that the annual Olympics (spelled Olympicks in Dover's day) once attracted crowds in excess of 30,000. The local Olympics have started up again, but with a little more concern for the health of the competitors – shin kicking is definitely out, for example. But there is no nonsense about modern sports – here you will find good old-fashioned tug-of-war competitions, as well as skittles and wrestling.

The extensive plateau of Dover's Hill.

SECRETS

While you're there

Visit nearby **CHIPPING CAMPDEN**, one of the less-visited Cotswold towns but delightfully filled with splendid early buildings, pubs and hotels.

Secret place to stay

DORMY HOUSE HOTEL, Broadway, Worcestershire (dormyhouse.co.uk). A lovely old hotel and former farmhouse in a picture-postcard setting complete with glorious views across open countryside.

Brean Down

SOMERSET

Brean Down is a spectacular limestone peninsula that runs for 2.4km (1½ miles) out into the Bristol Channel at the western end of the Mendips. Formerly an island, it is connected to the mainland by about a 1km (900yd)-strip of salt marsh. The down is surrounded by steep cliffs and rocky foreshore, and it is both a Site of Special Scientific Interest and a Scheduled Ancient Monument. With wide views, fascinating archaeology and absorbing geological and wildlife interest, Brean Down is unique, its value enhanced by the fact that so few people visit it.

At the extreme seaward end of the down there is Palmerston Fort, built in 1865 and then adapted and reused during World War II. This, like Brean Down itself, is now looked after by the National Trust. The great radio pioneer Marconi carried out a number of experiments here in 1897 transmitting radio signals across the Bristol Channel to and from Brean Down.

Brean Down has been inhabited for thousands of years – there are Bronze Age barrows and Iron Age field systems, as well as a Roman temple. Early Christian remains were found here. Today the down is populated by a rich diversity of wildlife. Many migrant birds make their first landfall here, including brambling, redpoll and red bunting. Among the plants are rock samphire and sea lavender, white rockrose and Somerset hair-grass. The open grassland is home to delicate chalk-blue butterflies and dark-green fritillaries.

View across to Brean Down.

SECRETS

While you're there

Visit the remarkable Victorian family estate at **TYNTESFIELD**, Wraxall, recently restored to its former Victorian grandeur. Includes house, chapel, gardens and woodland (nationaltrust.org.uk).

Secret place to stay

WOODLANDS COUNTRY HOUSE HOTEL. Brent Knoll (woodlands-hotel.co.uk). ☎ 01278 760232. Just 8km (5 miles) from Brean Down, set in 1.6ha (4 acres) of gardens.

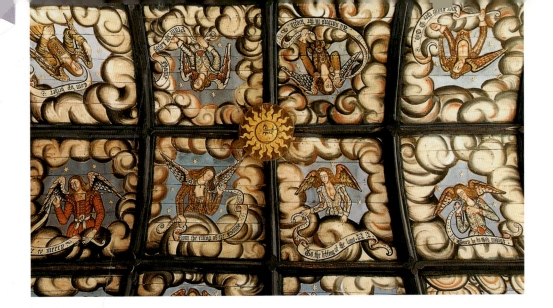

Muchelney Abbey

SOMERSET

The lavishly decorated ceiling in the abbot's house has been restored to its former splendour.

Founded by the Wessex King Ine, the monastery at Muchelney was destroyed in Viking raids and then rebuilt in the 10th century. The dissolution of the monasteries in the 16th century resulted in the destruction of this beautifully situated Benedictine foundation. Most of the monastic structures were plundered for building materials and the abbot's house only survived because it was reused as a farmhouse.

The church has a painted ceiling, and nearby is the beautiful thatched medieval priest's house, which is open to the public. Muchelney means 'big island' and when the rains and floods come Muchelney becomes an island again, as it would have been 1000 years before the monks drained the land round about and built their carp ponds and closed communities.

SECRETS

MUCHELNEY ABBEY, Langport, Somerset, TA10 0DQ (english-heritage.org.uk). Check website for opening times. Price: adult £4.20, child £2.50.

While you're there

Visit STEMBRIDGE TOWER MILL, High Ham ☎ 01935 823289. This is the last remaining thatched mill in Britain and its high location offers spectacular views across the surrounding countryside.

Secret place to stay

ASH HOUSE COUNTRY HOTEL, Martock (ashhousehotel.co.uk). ☎ 01935 822036. A beautiful Georgian country house located in the heart of the peaceful Somerset countryside.

Burrow Mump

SOMERSET

The Somerset Levels once covered hundreds of square kilometres of waterlogged swamp, which were filled with wildfowl and waders. It was inhabited by isolated groups of hardy individuals who eked out a living by weaving baskets from the willows that grow abundantly in the area, catching eels and other fish, and trapping birds. Much of the Levels have been drained, but the flat landscape – reminiscent of the East Anglian fens – retains at least something of its ancient atmosphere.

Rising out of this wide, flat landscape is a solitary, little-visited hill known as Burrow Mump. At the top of the hill is a ruined church. It was here in 1645, at the height of the Civil War, that the defeated remnants of King Charles' army retreated after they were defeated at the nearby Battle of Langport. They were pursued by the Parliamentarians and finally routed.

The church on the mump was rebuilt in the 18th century, but never completed, and the ruins were beautified in the early 19th century to make an attractive folly – a sort of fake antique building more often found in the grounds of great estates.

Burrow Mump has been owned by the National Trust for more than half a century. It has associations with nearby Athelney, where King Alfred is said to have held court, and it offers the most glorious views from its summit – out across the levels as far as Glastonbury Tor some 16km (10 miles) away.

The ruined church on Burrow Mump.

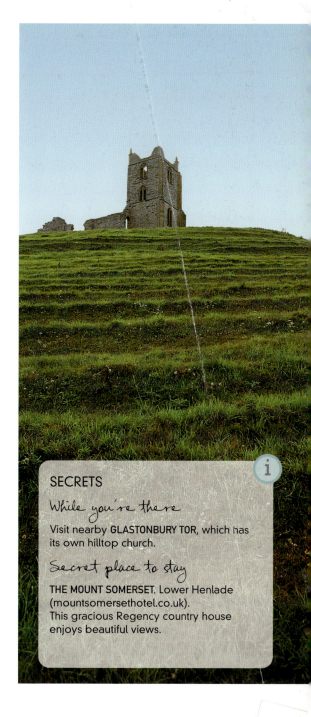

SECRETS

While you're there

Visit nearby **GLASTONBURY TOR**, which has its own hilltop church.

Secret place to stay

THE MOUNT SOMERSET. Lower Henlade (mountsomersethotel.co.uk). This gracious Regency country house enjoys beautiful views.

Caen Hill Locks

WILTSHIRE

This is an extraordinary piece of Georgian engineering that deserves to be far better known. The Kennet and Avon Canal, running from Bradford-on-Avon to Newbury, is an 140km (87 mile) stretch of waterway. The challenge facing engineer John Rennie was how to enable the canal to travel up the side of a hill on the outskirts of Devizes. So many

SECRETS

While you're there

Visit the market town of **DEVIZES**, where the flight of locks end. The small town has some lovely old buildings including 16th-century shops, a castle and pubs.

Secret place to stay

THE BLACK SWAN HOTEL, Devizes (blackswandevizes.co.uk). Unpretentious, pretty and reasonably priced.

steps were needed in the steep-sided hill that he could not provide the normal flight-of-locks system, which would have involved building a lock followed by a basin followed by a lock, each directly above the other. Because Rennie's locks – completed in 1810 – had to be so close together, he had the brilliant idea of building the basins at the sides of the locks to hold enough water to allow them to work – and these side basins can still be seen today, though the series is no longer complete.

This part of the Kennet and Avon Canal was in use until just before World War II. The remarkable flight of locks was in danger of being lost forever as dereliction set in, and it was only after a massive and lengthy work of restoration that the locks were returned to full working order and reopened in 1990. A total of 29 locks climb the hill, but central to this great work of engineering is the spectacular Caen Hill flight of 16, which run in a straight line up the hillside.

The Caen Hill flight is a daunting sight for pleasure boaters.

St John the Baptist Church WILTSHIRE

A delightful rural church just south of the river Thames on the northern fringe of Wiltshire, St John the Baptist is largely 13th century. The glory of this church at Inglesham is its wealth of medieval and earlier wall paintings. The earliest of these is a painting on the south wall depicting Mary and Jesus being blessed by the Hand of God, and thought to be Saxon in origin. There are groups of paintings covering the 13th to the early 19th century, in some cases overlapping each other and up to seven layers thick. One of the most prominent is a 14th-century Doom (Last Judgement) in the north aisle.

The interior is filled with original 17th- and 18th-century box pews, and a pulpit of similar age. The small chancel is separated from the nave by a wooden 15th-century screen. The interior is blissfully unaltered and would likely be recognized instantly by a 17th-century parishioner.

An unassuming exterior hides internal glory.

One of the reasons that Inglesham church remains so unspoilt is probably down to the intervention of William Morris, the Arts and Crafts movement pioneer. Morris lived at Kelmscott, a short distance away, and led a restrained programme of restoration in 1888 that kept the medieval character of the church largely intact.

SECRETS

While you're there

Visit **LECHLADE-ON-THAMES** less than a mile away. Often overlooked, this pretty market town has some beautiful old houses, and its bridge across the Thames still has its toll house.

Secret place to stay

THE NEW INN HOTEL, Lechlade-on-Thames (newinnhotel.co.uk). On the banks of the river, in a tranquil setting.

North Meadow

WILTSHIRE

Cricklade is an ancient village. The remains of a Saxon mint were found here by archaeologists, along with Roman and later remains. The village lies on the infant river Thames and was busy and prosperous during the Middle Ages. At the north end of the high street there is an extremely rare survivor. As most of lowland Britain's meadows were ploughed up, those pockets that remained grew ever smaller, until efforts were made to save the last few remaining. North Meadow, or Nar Mead as it is know locally, is one of these.

Just by the old stone bridge over the Thames you reach the ancient water meadow. In spring and summer it is a mass of rare and beautiful flowers, including the snake's head fritillary, which blooms in April – the presence of these rare flowers explains why the meadow has been a designated nature reserve since 1973. North Meadow's 45ha (112 acres) have never been sprayed with modern chemicals, or ploughed or damaged in any way. In medieval and earlier times 'right holders' in the village grazed their animals on the mead between 12 August and 12 February.

The word 'meadow' has the same meaning as old church 'lammas' meaning 'harvest festival', (from loaf mass) land.

North Meadow is full of snake's head fritillaries in late spring.

SECRETS

While you're there

Visit **CRICKLADE** itself, a remarkably quiet unspoilt town well off the beaten track. The straight road along which the town is built was set out by Alfred the Great.

Secret place to stay

STANTON HOUSE HOTEL, Stanton Fitzwarren (stantonhouse.co.uk). An elegant stone house overlooking Stanton lake and park.

Malmesbury Abbey WILTSHIRE

The mostly 12th-century remains of this once remote abbey represent only about one-third of the original abbey buildings. The church originally had a spire taller than that at Salisbury Cathedral but it collapsed early in the 16th century. When Henry VIII closed all the monasteries, a local man – one William Stump – bought the monastery and decided to convert it into the parish church, a move that ensured the survival of this wonderful building.

Malmsbury is said to be the place where the Cotswolds meets the West Country, and its former importance can be judged by the fact that Athelstan (895–939), the first king of a united England, is buried here. The mid-12th-century south porch through which visitors enter today is a splendid piece of Norman work, and there is a superb vaulted roof above the nave.

A sizeable chunk of Malmesbury Abbey survives.

SECRETS

While you're there

Don't miss the wonderful, carved 15th-century **MARKET CROSS** in the town of Malmesbury itself.

Secret place to stay

THE OLD BELL, Malmesbury (oldbellhotel.co.uk). Luxury and history combine to make a memorable stay. This hotel claims to be the oldest in England.

Silbury Hill

WILTSHIRE

Silbury Hill is one of the strangest structures in the world – it looks like a hill but is entirely manmade. There is no obvious explanation as to why it was built, which may be the reason why this earthwork is not better known.

The effort involved in building it without modern tools must have been prodigious. Conical and undamaged despite the passage of more than 3,000 years, the hill stands in the middle of the Wiltshire Plain near Marlborough. It is estimated that the amount of soil and rubble moved to make the hill rivals that moved to create the Great Pyramid at Giza – one estimate reckons 500 men working continuously seven days a week for 15 years could only just have completed the work.

It's been said that the mound was a colossal grave for a great Neolithic king but no evidence of burial has been found by archaeologists; others claim the hill is some kind of a sundial or zodiacal indicator, but again there is no basis for this suggestion. The archaeology that has been uncovered indicates that the hill began as a 6m (20ft) mound, which was later capped with chalk rubble and then increased dramatically to its present 40m (130ft) height by excavating a 7.5m (25ft) deep ditch all the way around and adding the excavated material to the top. Silbury completely covers slightly more than 2.25ha (5½ acres) of ground.

Silbury Hill dominates the Wiltshire Plain.

ⓘ

SECRETS

While you're there

Visit nearby **AVEBURY**, where this quaint old village is cut through by an ancient stone circle known as Avebury Henge.

Secret place to stay

THE LODGE, Avebury (aveburylodge.co.uk). Vegetarian B&B with a warm and comfortable feel.

Maud Heath's Causeway WILTSHIRE

Maud Heath was an extraordinary woman who in 1474 bequeathed her land in order that a solid path from the village of East Tytherton, where she lived, to Chippenham, the nearest market town 5km (3 miles) away, could be built. She wanted to ensure that the people of her village, could walk comfortably and dry-shod to the town over the marshlands.

The causeway that bears her name goes from Wick Hill through East Tytherton, crosses the Kennet and Avon Canal (not built of course until the early 19th century) and the river Avon, before running on past Langley Burrel to Chippenham. Much of the land along the route was low lying and flooded regularly in the Middle Ages. For much of its length today the causeway is just a raised path but the section at Kellaways – rebuilt early in the 19th century – shows how it must once have looked throughout its length.

The Kellaways section of the raised Causeway.

SECRETS

While you're there

Don't miss the pretty village of EAST TYTHERTON, which sits snugly in this ancient and glorious landscape.

Secret place to stay

BEECHFIELD HOUSE HOTEL AND RESTAURANT, Beanacre (beechfieldhouse.co.uk). Delightful and luxurious Victorian country house hotel that is easy to find and just 13km (8 miles) away.

Around 1.5m (5ft) high, it was originally supported by 64 brick arches. The causeway is still maintained by a committee of trustees who have met every year for 500 years. Maud Heath had sufficient presence of mind to leave money for maintaining the causeway, and today this investment still brings in something in the region of £100,000 a year. A pillar placed at the river crossing at Kellaways in 1698 explains Maud's story and there is a Georgian statue of her in bonnet and shawl at Wick Hill.

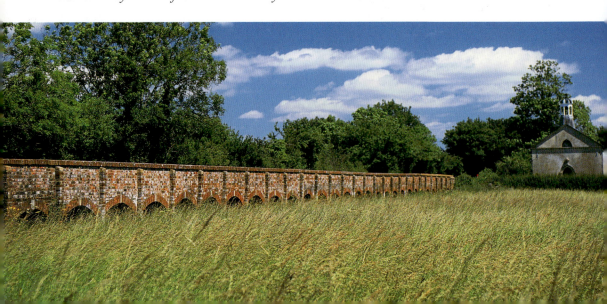

St Laurence's Church WILTSHIRE

Debate rages about the exact construction date of this extraordinary little church in Bradford-on-Avon, which, until just over a century ago, was thought to be just another old house! Stylistically, it looks as though it was built in the early 11th century but other evidence – most notably written – suggests a date sometime early in the 8th century.

St Laurence's is very lucky still to be with us. It must have ceased to be used as a church in the late Middle Ages. Certainly by the early 18th century the nave was being used as a school, while the chancel had been converted into a house, with two floors inserted into the tall building.

Canon Jones, the local vicar, began to investigate the buildings in the 1850s, and from his researches – and specifically from a reference in William of Malmesbury's (a notable 12th-century historian) *Gesta Pontificum* of 1125 – he concluded that this altered building was actually extremely ancient. William of Malmesbury had described how 'to this day there exists a little church which Aldhelm caused to have built to the name of the most blessed St Laurence'. Canon Jones continued to press for the return of the former church to ecclesiastical use and in 1871 it was bought and reconsecrated to St Laurence.

St Laurence's Church is rather high in relation to its ground dimensions. It has a small nave and an eastern chancel. Originally built without windows (these were added toward the end of the Saxon era), it has two angels – dated to about 950 – carved on each side of the arch.

St Laurence's contains fine 10th-century carvings.

SECRETS

While you're there

Visit the **BRIDGE TEA ROOMS**, consistently judged the best tea shop in Britain and serving generous portions of good food. (thebridgeatbradford.co.uk).

Secret place to stay

WOOLLEY GRANGE, Wooley Green (woolleygrangehotel.co.uk). Just 5km (3 miles) away, this Jacobean house offers facilities for children and a friendly welcome for dogs.

The Peto Garden

WILTSHIRE

Harold Peto, of Huguenot descent and an architect by profession, created this extraordinary Italian garden between 1899 and 1933 in the grounds of Iford Manor. Its importance can be judged by the fact that it is listed Grade I, and yet it is not nearly as well known as it should be. It is a romantic garden built to reflect the sort of sunny hillside gardens typical of Italy – wherever you go there are terraces, ponds, broad walks, little groups of mature trees, sculpture (much of it collected on Peto's travels) and wonderful vistas out across the countryside.

The garden contains many specimens that have survived from Peto's own first planting scheme – these include wisterias, cypresses and scented lilies. The house attached to the garden (not open to visitors) is almost as interesting – medieval in origin, it has, like so many English country houses, a classical façade added in the 18th century. In late spring it is draped with the flowers of magnificent wisteria.

The 1ha (2½-acre) garden includes the loggia, the great terrace and the Cloisters – a building in which operas are performed each summer. Among Peto's professional admirers the general view seems to be that he brilliantly combined the formal and informal in this unique garden, which should be on every tourist's list of places to visit.

The intimate Peto Garden features many pathways lined with statues.

SECRETS

PETO GARDEN at Iford Manor, Bradford-on-Avon, Wiltshire, BA15 2BA (ifordmanor.co.uk). ☎ 01225 863146. Open: Garden Apr Sun (& BH Mon) 14.00–17.00; May–Sep Tues–Thurs, Sat, Sun (& BH Mon) 14.00–17.00; Oct Sun & BH Mon 14.00–17.00. Price: adult £5, children visit free.

While you're there

Visit **DYRHAM PARK**, Dyrham, near Bath, South Gloucestershire (nationaltrust.org.uk). Late 17th-century house set in a deer park.

Secret place to stay

LANSDOWN GROVE HOTEL, Bath ☎ 01225 483888. Just a few miles away, the Lansdown is grand-looking and reasonably priced.

Cherhill Down

WILTSHIRE

Cherhill rises high above the Wiltshire Plain and is topped by the splendid 38m (125ft)-high Lansdowne Monument, a stone obelisk built in 1845. Designed by Sir Charles Barry on behalf of the third Marquess of Lansdowne, the monument commemorates William Petty (1623–87), who rose from humble beginnings to become Surgeon General to Oliver Cromwell and one of the wealthiest men in England. Petty's daughter married the third son of the Marquis. Below the monument are the remains of an Iron Age earthwork known as Oldbury Castle.

The white horse and the Petty monument.

Pepperbox Hill

WILTSHIRE

A little-known octagonal two-floored brick tower that looks rather like a mellow 18th-century folly, the Pepperbox sits high on Brickworth Down, commanding wide views across to east and west. The tower was built in 1606 by Giles Eyre for reasons that remain obscure – one suggestion is that it was a place from which local landowners' wives could watch the hunt (presumably the hunt only ever circled the hill!) without exposing themselves to the public gaze. The tower gets its name from the simple fact that it looks like a 17th-century pepperpot.

Apart from the Pepperbox, the h deserves to be better known because of a series of experiments carried out here by Guglielmo Marconi in 1896, during one of which he managed to send a signal to Pepperbox Hill from 6km (4 miles) away – the rest, as they say, is history.

Pepperbox Hill enjoyed its greatest fame – or notoriety – in the early 18th century when it was apparently a haunt of highwaymen, who attacked carriages just as they reached the top of the hill. The carriages were at their most vulnerable at this point because the horses were too tired from their climb to run away!

The Pepperbox has always provided good views, but no one knows quite what was being viewed!

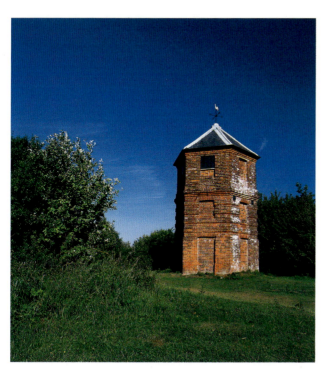

SECRETS

While you're there

Visit the **CATHEDRAL CLOSE** at Salisbury. One of the loveliest streets in Britain, it will transport you back in time to a more gentle era of English history with its enclosed historic buildings that were built to house the clergy, and in close proximity to the impressive Cathedral.

Secret place to stay

BAT AND BALL INN, Breamore, just outside Salisbury ☎ 01725 512252. The whole village of Breamore is Tudor and well worth a visit. The Bat and Ball is a famous angler's inn.

ENGLAND

South East

IT MIGHT BE the most densely populated part of the country but the South East still has its quiet unspoilt corners, its ancient houses and remote villages. Here you will find the best of them, from Rudyard Kipling's lovely house at Burwash to the national rose collection at Mottisfont Abbey. In London you can visit an Elizabethan manor house or an unspoilt 17th-century coaching inn. In Berkshire you'll find gems such as the Ankerwycke Yew, one of Britain's most extraordinary trees, and in Surrey enjoy Chatley Heath Semaphore Tower. Wherever you go you'll find something wonderful to see – and somewhere comfortable to stay.

The Swiss Garden

BEDFORDSHIRE

The Swiss Garden, with its wandering peacocks and curious alpine feel, really does deserve to be better known – its 4ha (10 acres) are home to a mix of flowers, rare trees and garden architecture that reflect precisely the taste of the early 19th century, or more precisely that period in the 1820s when the craze for all things Swiss was at its height.

Rare trees and shrubs surround a maze of wandering paths that circle ponds or cross them via elaborate wrought-iron bridges. In the centre of what is essentially an alpine garden is the delightful little thatched Swiss Cottage from which the garden gets its name. In addition to the cottage there is, what our 18th-century ancestors would probably have called, a ferny grotto – it's a sort of dark cave lit occasionally by streaks of light from outside, and all very mysterious in a slightly contrived way.

The Swiss Garden was the creation of Lord Ongley and it is the best example we have of the Victorian idea of a typical Swiss garden. The architect of the garden buildings was probably John Buonarotti Papworth (1775–1847), who suggested that unpeeled bark should be used as cladding to give a genuine rustic look!

The Swiss Cottage surrounded by daffodils.

SECRETS

SWISS GARDEN, The Shuttleworth Collection, Shuttleworth (Old Warden) Aerodrome, nr Biggleswade, Bedfordshire, SG18 9EP (shuttleworth.org/swiss-garden/). ☎ 01767 627927. Open: Mar–Oct 9.30–17.00; Nov–Feb 9.30–16.00. Price: adult £5, child free.

While you're there

Visit the **MOOT HALL** in nearby Elstow ☎ 01234 266889. Now a small museum of 17th-century artefacts, the building dates back to the 16th century. Opening times vary and there is a small entrance fee.

Secret place to stay

BARNS HOTEL, Bedford (barnshotelbedford.co.uk). ☎ 01234 270044. Situated in a wonderful waterside location.

Bromham Mill

BEDFORDSHIRE

Bromham Mill on the river Ouse has been grinding corn for centuries. Set in 3ha (7 acres) of water meadows and near the remarkable Georgian 26-arch Bromham Bridge, it is a glorious glimpse of how England used to be, in a county that tends to be neglected by visitors heading for more exotic regions.

There has been a mill here since Saxon times, but the current picturesque building dates to the end of the 17th century, with Georgian and Victorian additions. It's a lovely mix of stonework, old brick and

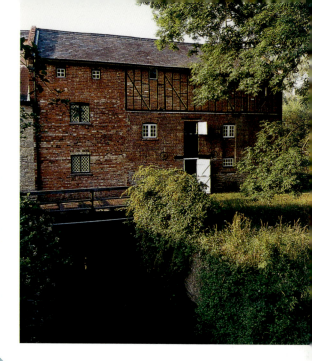

Bromham Mill dates from the 1600s.

timber framing. Originally there were two undershot wheels, but an iron breastwheel (installed in 1908) now provides the power for the wooden cogs and wheels. Watching them in operation is like looking back at the finest technology of an earlier age – the notches on the great wheel all had to be cut and fitted by hand. The mechanism is an extraordinary monument to the skills of long-dead craftsmen.

The mill and the buildings that once surrounded it – blacksmith's shop, piggery and several cottages – were once a self-sufficient community. A great eel trap by the waterwheel is recorded as having taken more than a hundredweight (51kg/112lb) of eels in one night. The apple orchard provided food as well as the right kind of timber for the gear teeth on the mill wheels.

BROMHAM MILL • BEDFORDSHIRE

Wrest Park

BEDFORDSHIRE

The Earls of Kent – the de Grey family – lived at Wrest Park for nearly 600 years. In that time they built three houses on the same site. The last, a French chateau built in 1834, is now home to the National Institute of Agricultural Engineering, but visitors can see the state rooms.

The real hidden treasures at Wrest Park, however, are the 36ha (90 acres) of gardens and the domed pleasure pavilion, designed in the baroque style by Thomas Archer (c.1668–1743). The pavilion has a magnificent set of early 18th-century wall paintings by the French artist Louis Hauduroy. The trompe l'oeil paintings, featuring mythological figures, coats-of-arms and monumental classical pillars, are the only example of Hauduroy's work on public view in England.

The 19th-century chateau at Wrest Park.

Flitton Church

BEDFORDSHIRE

It is curious how small, apparently ordinary churches sometimes conceal remarkable architectural gems. Flitton Church, dedicated to St John the Baptist, is a case in point. With its three-stage tower and curious castellations – which continue right round the building – the 15th-century church, built in a rich local sandstone, has the look of a short and stocky castle.

Adjoining the church is the 17th-century white stucco de Grey Mausoleum – also with castellations – a chancel filled with the monuments of one family. The earliest of these is to Sir Henry de Grey, who died in 1545. Apart from Sir Henry all the monuments – and they span three centuries continuing into Victorian times – are in white marble. They include Henry, the ninth earl (died 1651) and his wife Amabella, who died in 1658. The Henry who died in 1748 is portrayed in Roman dress. The de Grey family lived at nearby Wrest Park and their devotion to the family mausoleum is remarkable and unmatched anywhere else. The church is also remarkable as the last resting place of Thomas Hill, who died, we are assured, in 1601 at the grand old age of 128!

The many magnificent marble monuments of the de Grey family are the glory of St John the Baptist Church in Flitton.

SECRETS

While you're there

Visit **ST PETER'S CHURCH**, Flitwick, with its wonderful Norman font and door – a rare survival and little visited.

Secret place to stay

MENZIES FLITWICK MANOR HOTEL, Flitwick (menzies-hotels.co.uk/hotels/woburn-hotels/woburn-hotel-flitwick). A lovely Georgian building.

St Mary's Church

St Mary's Church in its tranquil setting.

BERKSHIRE

The tiny church of St Mary's, in the hilltop village of Aldworth on the Berkshire Downs, hides an extraordinary secret – the so-called Aldworth giants. Hidden away inside a church that you might easily pass by without a thought is the most magnificent set of 14th-century monuments in Britain. All the effigies were placed here for the de la Beche family, probably in the 1340s. They were almost certainly commissioned by Nicholas de la Beche, the lord of the manor, who lived at nearby (and long vanished) La Beche Castle.

The nine reclining effigies (which were damaged during the Civil War at a time when many churches became the focus of vandalism) completely dominate the church: two male figures lie under the arches of the south wall; between them is a figure that is believed to be Joan de la Beche, wife of Sir Philip. Sir Nicholas himself lies in the middle of the church with his head resting on a shield and wearing a helmet. Sir John and Isabelle de la Beche lie at the entrance to the chancel, and against the north wall is another John, as well as Sir Robert and the oversized giant figure of Philip de la Beche.

Outside the church is an ancient yew that was probably planted about the time the church was built in the 12th century.

SECRETS

While you're there

Visit nearby **GORING** where the Thames is squeezed through a natural gorge – the Goring Gap – and the Icknield Way meets the Ridgeway Path. A delightful place to spend an hour or two.

Secret place to stay

JOHN BARLEYCORN PUB AND HOTEL (thejohnbarleycornpub.co.uk). ☎ 01491 872509. Goring on Thames' best-kept secret.

Ankerwycke Yew

BERKSHIRE

The Ankerwycke Yew is one of the most extraordinary trees in Britain, but its significance is often overlooked because this remarkable tree grows at Runnymede (from rune mede meaning 'the place for meetings'). The location is the place where the Magna Carta, that great first charter limiting the powers of the monarch, was signed in 1215. Several centuries later the tree may also have witnessed the meetings of King Henry VIII with Anne Boleyn.

The tree, which still puts out leaves each spring, is far older than Magna Carta

SECRETS

ANKERWYCKE YEW, Runnymede, Old Windsor, Berkshire, SL4 2JL (nationaltrust.org.uk).

While you're there

Visit the **HOME PARK** at nearby Windsor. A lovely riverside park where an Isambard Kingdom Brunel railway bridge still crosses the Thames.

Secret place to stay

INN KEEPER'S LODGE, Old Windsor ☎ 0845 1126 104. Functional, but great if you're on a budget.

or anything else nearby. Scientists and conservationists are convinced that it is at least 2,500 years old. Certainly it has outlasted the priory whose medieval ruins are close by. Despite its great age and remarkable dimensions this stately yew was threatened in the 20th century by developers, who planned to cut it down in order to build a golf course; somehow this insanity was prevented and the tree is now protected and managed by the National Trust, who also maintain the historic meadows. Some historians now think that because the tree was already so old in the 13th century it may have been chosen as a suitable place under which to sign the famous charter. Yew trees are associated with places of worship and often grow surrounding churches.

The Ankerwycke Yew has an impressive 9.4m (31ft) girth.

Finchampstead Ridges BERKSHIRE

Finchampstead Ridges, with their lovely views across Hampshire and Surrey, deserve to be better known. Ancient pines and heather typify the ridges, which seem almost to float above the south-facing slopes of the Blackwater Valley.

On the northern slope is Simon's Wood. Both the wood and ridges are rare remnants of ancient heathland and they provide a home for numerous, sometimes rare plants and animals – here you may see siskin and spotted flycatcher, as well as woodlark, robin and blackbird. Rare plants include purple moor grass and marsh pennywort.

Finchampstead Ridges provide pleasant walks.

SECRETS

While you're there

Visit **ST JAMES' CHURCH**, Finchampstead, a fine 12th-century parish church with many Norman features and a glorious stained glass window.

Secret place to stay

TYLNEY HALL HOTEL, Hook, Hampshire (tylneyhall.co.uk). It is a dozen or so miles away but has a wonderful restaurant and comfortable rooms.

Paths weave in and out of this beautiful yet quiet valley, which has something of the desolate air of earlier times. At the bottom of the valley slope is Spout Pond, a refuge for once common, but now threatened, species of frog and toad. The pond also provides a home to numerous colourful species of damselfly and dragonfly.

Waddesdon Manor

BUCKINGHAMSHIRE

Built in the French Renaissance style between 1874 and 1889, from the outside the house is a fake chateau, but the inside reveals a very different story. Waddesdon was built for a family that was, and still is, one of the richest in the world: the Rothschilds. Baron Ferdinand de Rothschild, who commissioned the house, was a passionate Francophile – hence the

An ornate water feature at Waddesdon Manor.

extraordinary chateau-style exterior – who filled Waddesdon with countless works of art and pictures. The magnificent and priceless collection includes Sèvres porcelain, Savonnerie carpets, Beauvais tapestries and furniture made for the French royal family. English works of art include pictures by Gainsborough and Reynolds. There are also masterpieces by 17th-century Flemish and Dutch painters, as well as a superb collection of arms and armour.

The Victorian gardens are equally precious – with superb displays of bedding plants, a parterre, knot garden and numerous exotic trees. Managed and preserved to a high standard by the National Trust, there is plenty here to keep you entertained.

SECRETS

WADDESDON MANOR, Waddesdon, near Aylesbury, Buckinghamshire, HP18 0JH (nationaltrust.org.uk). ☎ 01296 653226. Check website for opening times. Price: House and gardens weekends adult £17, child £13. Gardens weekends: adult £8, child £4.50. All visitors require a timed ticket for the house, bookable up to 24 hours in advance.

While you're there

Visit the nearby **HUGHENDEN MANOR**, High Wycombe (nationaltrust.org.uk). Home of the great Victorian prime minister Benjamin Disraeli.

Secret place to stay

SPREAD EAGLE, Thame, Oxfordshire (spreadeaglethame.co.uk). This ancient house was made famous in the 1930s when innkeeper John Fothergill wrote a book about his years here. It is perfectly placed to explore the county.

Ivinghoe Beacon

BUCKINGHAMSHIRE

It is hard to believe that somewhere as spectacular as Ivinghoe Beacon can exist so close to London. But here, just half an hour's drive north of one of the most densely populated cities on earth, is a hilltop with breathtaking views across much of southern England. With its Iron Age hill fort, Ivinghoe is actually part of one of the National Trust's biggest estates, known as Ashridge, which runs right along the Chilterns through Hertfordshire and Buckinghamshire. The estate is an impressive mixture of heathland, downland, ancient woodland common and open hilltop. Much of it is a designated Site of Special Scientific Interest.

Once the downland of the beacon was grazed by sheep, which gave it a distinct cropped look. The sheep largely vanished in the 1930s and have only been reintroduced recently in an attempt to restore the hilltop to its earlier state.

When you've enjoyed the breathtaking views there is much nearby to enjoy, from ancient pollarded trees at Frithsden to the sunken droveways below the beacon itself. The estate woodland, heath and common are home to many rare species of plant and animal, including sparrowhawk, woodcock, firecrest and tawny owl. On the slopes below the beacon you might be lucky enough to see the Duke of Burgundy fritillary butterfly.

Looking toward the Iron Age fort.

SECRETS

While you're there

Why not enjoy walking a few miles of **THE RIDGEWAY PATH**, which begins close to Ivinghoe? Now a national trail, it was once an ancient trade route.

Secret place to stay

BELLOWS MILL, Dunstable (www.bellowsmill.co.uk). An ancient waterside mill.

Claydon House

BUCKINGHAMSHIRE

Claydon House is a jewel in the National Trust's crown. The house was built by the second Lord Verney in 1768, or rather, the house as it exists today was the recreation of a much earlier home, which was intended to be palatial in size and style. A huge west wing was built and intensions were to build a twin wing that would be connected through a rotunda, though it was never completed. What remains today is just one section of the original house, which is filled with rooms decorated, in what was at the time, the first flowering of a passion for all things oriental. The interior is uniquely beautiful and

Claydon House, home of the Verney family.

SECRETS

CLAYDON HOUSE, Middle Claydon, nr Buckingham, Buckinghamshire, MK18 2EY (nationaltrust.org.uk). ☎ 01296 730349. Check the website for opening times. Price: adult £6.80, child £3.35, family £17.25. The gardens are not owned by the National Trust and incur an additional fee, if you wish to visit them too.

While you're there

Visit the **KING'S HEAD**, Aylesbury (nationaltrust.org.uk). One of the loveliest inns in Britain and dating back to 1455.

Secret place to stay

HORWOOD HOUSE, Little Horwood (horwoodhousemiltonkeynes.com). An interesting Victorian building with remarkable and extensive grounds.

extraordinary. The main motifs of the decorative scheme are pagodas, oriental birds and exquisite summerhouses. The decoration includes some of the best woodcarving in Europe. The 18th-century craftsman responsible for the work was Luke Lightfoot, whose intricate figures will stand comparison with almost anything created by the hand of Grinling Gibbons.

Claydon, which is set in its own park, is said to be haunted. One of the ghosts is said to be Florence Nightingale – a relative of the Verney family – she was a frequent visitor. Mementoes of her life can be seen in the room in which she slept.

The park sweeps down to three beautiful lakes, the home of giant bronze-coloured carp and fearsome pike.

West Wycombe Caves BUCKINGHAMSHIRE

Sir Francis Dashwood and a number of his aristocratic friends set up what was known as the Hell Fire Club in the mid-18th century. The club met in the former chalk mines to the west of West Wycombe. Other Hell Fire Clubs certainly existed, but this was the best known precisely because its members – aristocrats to a man – were so well bred. Dashwood's club had originally been known as the Monks of Medmenham because they met at the abbey of Medmenham on the Thames, but when that was destroyed by fire they had to find a new home.

The club is reputed to have become involved in all sorts of devilish activities – such as orgies and lengthy drinking bouts – but worst of all, from the authorities' point of view, the club was a haven for free-masonry and free thinking.

The caves where Dashwood's rakes once met are chalk, but flint rich, and were almost certainly mined in prehistoric times. Sir Francis had them enlarged in the 1740s to provide work for local unemployed men and, of course, to provide a meeting place for fellow club members. Today the caves, which extend to 98m (330ft) below ground, are pretty much as they were in Dashwood's time, with the modern addition of life-sized waxworks in 18th-century costume. When you walk through the caves – including the huge banqueting hall – it is extraordinary to think that they were all dug by hand.

The Hellfire Caves were once mined.

SECRETS

WEST WYCOMBE CAVES, Church Lane, West Wycombe, Buckinghamshire, HP14 3AH (hellfirecaves.co.uk). Open: Apr–Oct 11.00–17.30; Nov–Mar Sat, Sun, BH & school hol 11.00–dusk. Price: adult £5, child & NT members £4, family £15.

While you're there

Visit **ST LAWRENCE CHURCH** at West Wycombe, once described as the loveliest church in England.

Secret place to stay

GEORGE AND DRAGON, West Wycombe (georgeanddragonhotel.com). An old inn in the centre of town with a feel far removed from any chain hotel. It's also supposed to be haunted!

Coombe Hill

BUCKINGHAMSHIRE

Coombe Hill, the highest point on the Chilterns, is a spectacular hilltop within easy reach of London. It's the sort of place you would expect to find in some more remote rural location, not on the edge of one of the world great conurbations.

From the top of the hill, the Aylesbury Valley and the long ridge of the Chilterns can be seen for mile upon mile on a good day. Woodland paths wind across the vast acreage owned by the National Trust and will take you through quiet woodlands and out across open ground if your inclination is to go walking. Sheep have been introduced as a management tool to control invasive scrub species, so this chalky downland looks much as it would have done in the 18th and earlier centuries when sheep were the mainstay of the economy.

The rich grassland environment is home to a myriad of species – harebells, wild thyme, vetch, wild strawberry and rock rose among them. On the flatter areas there are oaks and beech trees and in the nearby Low Scrubs area of wooded common, evidence remains of ancient coppice, for this was once common land where poor villagers could come to gather firewood.

On the summit of Coombe Hill is a monument to a conflict now largely forgotten – the Boer War. Erected in 1904, the elegant obelisk was destroyed by lightning in the 1930s before being restored. It had to be concealed in World War II to prevent it from being used as a marker by German aircraft!

SECRETS

While you're there

Visit the nearby enigmatic ruins of Norman **BERKHAMSTED CASTLE** (berkhamsted-castle.org.uk).

Secret place to stay

PENNYFARTHING HOTEL, Berkhamsted (thepennyfarthinghotel.co.uk). Small, friendly and right in the middle of this delightful old town.

COOMBE HILL • BUCKINGHAMSHIRE

Wicken Fen

CAMBRIDGESHIRE

A huge area of what is today East Anglia was once a forbidding wetland. Right across Cambridgeshire, Norfolk and Lincolnshire the land was permanently flooded and only the local people knew the routes through the treacherous bog and marsh. They made a living catching eels and other fish in baskets that they made themselves, and trapped wildfowl in winter. Then came the Dutch engineers and the marshes were drained and the floods began to recede; one of the greatest wildlife habitats in the world – an area that was once home to millions of birds, insects and mammals – became the flat, empty farmland we see today. Just a few tiny pockets of the old fen still exist, hidden amid tens of thousands of acres of arable land. The best of these is undoubtedly Wicken Fen.

Wicken is also Britain's oldest nature reserve. It was probably the Victorians' enthusiasm for collecting insects that saved Wicken from the draining that destroyed

The fens' last working wooden windpump.

SECRETS

While you're there

Visit **ISLEHAM PRIORY CHURCH** just a few miles away in the village of Isleham. A most remarkable building, this small Benedictine priory church escaped destruction at the dissolution, though was later converted for farm use.

Secret place to stay

LAMB HOTEL, Ely (thelambhotel-ely.co.uk). Right in the centre of this cathedral city, the 15th-century hotel is the perfect place to stay while you explore a town that was once an island in the fens.

the rest of the fens – the great Charles Darwin, among others, came here on several insect-collecting trips.

The reserve now covers more than 234ha (800 acres) and traditional fen practices – reed harvesting and peat cutting – have produced an extraordinary rich waterscape. Thirty species of mammal have been recorded, as well as more than 200 species of birds, 25 species of dragonfly, 1,000 species of beetle and more than 100 species of moths and butterflies.

Flag Fen

CAMBRIDGESHIRE

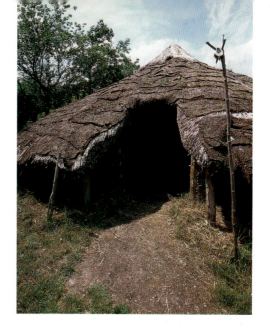

Recreated Bronze Age house at Flag Fen.

The stone and earthwork remains of pre-literate peoples in England – Stonehenge, Avebury and so on – represent only a small fraction of the artefacts that would have been made 2,000–3,000 or more years ago. There is no doubt that these ancient people, about whom we know so little, made many of their buildings, their tools, boats and utensils from timber, a material that only rarely survived long enough to be discovered by modern archaeologists.

Very occasionally we find vestiges of their extraordinary woodworking skills in odd fragments found in waterlogged sites, but it is very rare indeed to find a major site with large amounts of prehistoric wooden technology intact, yet that is just what was found at Flag Fen. Discovered as recently as 1982, Flag Fen is a remarkable place – a wooden platform the size of a modern football pitch was built here around BC3000 with 60,000 timber posts in alignment driven into the ground, yet we have almost no idea why this work was carried out at great expense of time and labour.

The timbers at Flag Fen are so well preserved in the waterlogged conditions that archaeologists can even determine the type of axes used to fell the trees and how many axes were probably used, as well as details of how the logs were split using wedges and then shaped. The museum at Flag Fen has on display the oldest wooden wheel ever found in England, together with other remarkable timber artefacts, swords and personal artefacts.

SECRETS

FLAG FEN BRONZE AGE CENTRE, The Droveway, Northey Road, Peterborough, Cambridgeshire, PE6 7QJ (vivacity-peterborough.com/museums-and-heritage/flag-fen/). ☎ 01733 313414. Open: Apr–Sept daily 10.00–17.00. Check website for winter opening times. Price: adult £5, child £3.75, family £13.75.

While you're there

The old town of **PETERBOROUGH** was mushroomed in size in the 1960s and 1970s as developers expanded the housing stock to alleviate a national shortage. The cathedral, which is at the heart of the town, remains a marvel of medieval art.

Secret place to stay

THE GOAT, Frognall (thegoatfrognall.com). An historic inn with real charm.

Wimpole Hall and Farm CAMBRIDGESHIRE

Wimpole is the largest country house in Cambridgeshire. The house was built in 1640, to replace an ancient moated house, and, as with so many English country houses, it has been added to over the centuries. Some of the best architects that the country has ever produced added their stamp to this landmark including James Gibbs, Henry Flitcroft, Sir John Soane, Humphry Repton and Lancelot 'Capability' Brown. Soane built the beautiful bathhouse, the book room and the extraordinary yellow drawing room.

Much of the furniture in the house was collected by Mrs Elsie Bambridge, the daughter of Rudyard Kipling, who bought the house in the 1930s and filled it with the type of furniture and pictures it would have had when the Earls of Hardwicke owned the house in the late 18th century. She made a splendid job of it too.

Set in more than 1,000ha (2,500 acres) of parkland, with landscaped gardens, miles of walks, and even a gothic tower, this is a gem of a place to visit. The grounds are rather eerie to walk through since the remains of the three medieval villages, which were destroyed to create the view from the house, can still be seen as bumps and hollows. The outlines of long-vanished lanes combine to make any walk through the grounds a ghostly experience.

Classical figures adorn Wimpole Hall.

SECRETS

WIMPOLE ESTATE, Arrington, Royston, Cambridgeshire, SG8 0BW (wimpole.org). Check website for times and prices.

While you're there
Visit the ROYSTON CAVE, Royston (roystoncave.co.uk). A unique manmade cavern with medieval wall carvings.

Secret place to stay
OLD BULL INN HOTEL, Royston (oldbullinn-royston.co.uk). The Old Bull will give you a taste of East Anglia as it once was.

Anglesey Abbey

CAMBRIDGESHIRE

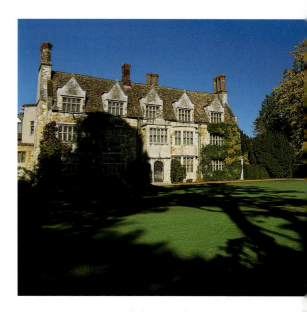

We don't know exactly when Anglesey Abbey was founded but it was almost certainly during the reign of Henry I, who died in 1135. By the mid-13th century it was a thriving religious community. When Henry VIII closed the abbey in 1535 with the dissolution of the monasteries it was not entirely demolished, which was unusual, but instead turned into a house. Today the Tudor house it became retains much of the original Augustinian chapter house and monks' parlour.

Anglesey Abbey, originally a priory, was transformed into a family home after the dissolution of the monasteries.

SECRETS

ANGLESEY ABBEY, Quy Road, Lode, Cambridge, CB25 9EJ (nationaltrust.org.uk). ☎ 01223 810080. Open: House Mar–Oct Wed–Sat 11.00–17.00. Garden 10.30–16.30. Price: House, garden and mill: adult £11, child £5, family £25, family (1 adult) £15. Garden and mill: adult £5.95, child £2.95, family £14.85, family (1 adult) £8.90.

While you're there

Don't miss the nearby **LODE WATERMILL**. It's on the Anglesey estate and is a lovely example of a now rare fenland building. Opening times and running times vary, so check the National Trust website.

Secret place to stay

THE WHITE HART INN, Fulbourn (whitehartfulbourn.co.uk). ☎ 01223 880264. Very reasonably priced, attractive, historic and quiet.

During the 17th century the house was owned by the Parker family – one member of this family was the wealthy mail carrier Thomas Hobson who coined the phrase 'Hobson's Choice' meaning, in effect, no choice. The house was also owned for a time by Sir George Downing (who built Downing Street in London), and then in 1926 by Huttlestone Broughton (Lord Fairhaven). He brought his huge collection of antiques to the house and set about transforming the 40ha (100 acre) garden into 22 distinct areas. These include a highly symmetrical formal garden, lawns and avenues of trees (which contain one of England's finest collections of garden statuary), snowdrop walks, a dahlia garden, a pinetum and a gorgeous arboretum with oaks, horse chestnut and lime trees.

Little Gidding

CAMBRIDGESHIRE

One of the most magical churches in England, Little Gidding may be a challenge to find as it lies just off a tiny road between Steeple Gidding and Great Gidding in Huntingdonshire.

The original ancient church was granted in 1185 to the Knights Templar of the Order of St John. They had hoped to use revenue from local tithes to help fund the crusades, but, for some curious reason that history does not record, no money was forthcoming. In 1348 disaster struck and Little Gidding, along with many other nearby villages, was struck by the plague. Within a short time the village was abandoned.

Three centuries later, by 1625 the estate into which the church was incorporated had passed into the hands of the Ferrar family, who were London merchants. The Ferrars settled here in the manor house, establishing a religious community. In total 40 people lived an almost monastic life of quiet and prayer here.

The church we see today was rebuilt in 1714 by John and Thomas Ferrar and still has its 18th-century benches. Little Gidding inspired the fourth of T. S. Eliot's *Four Quartets*. Eliot was moved by the beauty of the church's setting and its history of contemplative Christianity.

The area around Little Gidding is rich in ancient historical associations. There is evidence of Roman settlement and, from 500–700AD, an Anglo-Saxon community thrived here. The name 'Gidding' comes from 'Gydel', the name of a Saxon warlord who once owned the land.

The church in Cambridgeshire is a focus for pilgrims.

SECRETS

While you're there

Don't miss **GREAT AND STEEPLE GIDDING**. Both are tiny but surrounded by footpaths.

Secret place to stay

THE GEORGE, Stamford (georgehotelofstamford.com). It's a drive of about 24km (15 miles) but Stamford boasts one of the loveliest old hotels in England, timber-framed with crooked floors and ceilings.

Layer Marney Tower ESSEX

The gatehouse tower was intended as a grand entrance to a magnificent house, but the original owner died before the project was completed.

Visitors to Layer Marney often feel sad that the rest of the house appears to have been demolished, but in fact, it was never built. The huge gatehouse – the tallest Tudor gatehouse in the country at nearly 24m (80ft) – was originally intended as part of a courtyard house. The tower was commissioned by the first Lord Marney in the early part of the 16th century. His son continued the work, but died without heir soon after his father.

It is actually a twin tower with a gatehouse above the entrance in between the two towers. It has eight storeys of windows, is built from small, beautiful handmade bricks and is covered in heraldic and other carvings. These include dolphins and angels in softly coloured terracotta.

Today, still privately owned, the tower is open to visitors, as well as being licensed to conduct weddings. Visitors may climb the narrow winding staircase for spectacular view out across the wide flat landscape.

SECRETS

LAYER MARNEY TOWER, Layer Marney, nr Colchester, Essex, C05 9US (layermarneytower.co.uk). ☎ 01206 330784. Apr, May, Jun & Sep Sun & Wed 12.00–17.00; Jul & Aug Sun–Thurs 12.00–17.00. Price: adult £6, child £4, family £18.

While you're there

Visit **ST OSYTH PRIORY**. Partly ruined, but gradually being rescued by English Heritage, the priory is a wonderful group of more than 100 buildings dating back to monastic times. It is privately owned, but well worth seeing from a distance.

Secret place to stay

OLDE SWAN HOTEL, Brightlingsea (ye-olde-swan.com). ☎ 01206 302024. Reasonably priced, comfortable and the oldest building in a town that is well worth exploring in its own right.

SECRETS

THRIFT WOOD, Bicknacre (essexwt.org.uk/visitor_centres__nature_res erves/thrift_wood). Managed by Essex Wildlife Trust.

While you're there

Why not visit the **ANCIENT HUNTING FOREST** at Hatfield, which offers more than 400ha (1,000 acres) of woodland and pasture, two ornamental lakes and an 18th-century Shell House (nationaltrust.org.uk/hatfield forest).

Secret place to stay

THE BELL INN, (bell-inn.co.uk/). ☎ 01375 642563. An old coaching inn that is family run. Looks glorious in summer when the courtyard is filled with flowers.

Thrift Wood ESSEX

Ancient woodland is now very rare indeed in lowland England, which makes the survival of Thrift Wood all the more remarkable. Here, against all the odds, you will find almost 20ha (50 acres) of centuries-old oak alongside coppiced hornbeam, ash, chestnut and birch trees. The wood is also home to the heath fritillary butterfly, which became extinct in Essex in the early 1980s and was subsequently reintroduced.

Coppicing is still carried on here as it was in earlier centuries, and this management technique actually makes the site more attractive to a number of bird and plant species. Among a wide range of common and not so common birds are warblers and three species of woodpecker. A murky pond with boggy ground surrounding it provides a home for several species of amphibian, as well as moss, spearwort and sedges.

The trackways through the wood are thought to be sections of medieval green lanes, and as this area has never been ploughed you can be sure as you wander through it in summer that you are seeing Essex much as it might have looked to a traveller in the Middle Ages, for Essex was then one of the most heavily wooded regions of the country – it was the county from which the oaks were cut to build the fleet that defeated the Spanish Armada in 1588. Today only rare and hidden fragments like this remain to remind us of what was once here.

Sun-dappled Thrift Wood.

St Andrew's Church ESSEX

Timber, the favoured building material of Vikings and Saxons does not last – which may explain why in many cases we know far more about the architecture of the Romans (who built largely in stone) in Britain than about the timber-building invaders of the Dark Ages. But just outside Chipping Ongar, hardly any distance from London, and concealed down an unlikely looking track, stands what is almost certainly the oldest wooden church in the world – St Andrew's Church, Greensted, also known as Greensted Church.

The walls of this small church are made from whole split oak-tree trunks, probably incorporated into the building in the 11th century, but parts of the church have been dated to as early as 650AD. The Normans

The walls of the church are 11th century in part with many later renovations.

and Tudors added to the church and it has been restored and refitted many times over the years, but for some extraordinary reason those massive oak walls were never replaced. The curved side of each split log faces outward leaving the flat sides to create a more or less even surface on the inside of the church.

SECRETS

ST ANDREW'S CHURCH, Greensted (greenstedchurch.org.uk). Regular services are held here and guided tours may be arranged for those interested in the history.

While you're there

Visit the **CHURCH OF ST MARTIN OF TOURS** in nearby Chipping Ongar. It was partly built with reused Roman tiles and bricks.

Secret place to stay

SWAN HOTEL, Thaxted (swanhotel-thaxted.co.uk). This is a delight – with open fires, low-ceilinged bars and crooked floors and ceilings.

St Peter on the Wall ESSEX

If there were a prize for the loneliest seeming building in England, St Peter on the Wall would win it.

Miles from any house, St Peter stands at the mouth of the river Blackwater. It was built by St Cedd in the *c.*650AD using stone and brick from a nearby Roman fort that might well – just 200 years after the Romans left Britain – have been largely intact at the time that work began on the church. What we see today is the chapel. Throughout the Dark Ages it would have been part of a small group of monastic buildings that would have incorporated a hospital, library, school and farm and was home to men and women.

When the wind hurtles in from the North Sea this is a bitterly cold place, but St Cedd had travelled to Essex from the

The Saxon chapel was built on Roman ruins and can be reached via ancient footpaths.

world-famous monastery on Lindisfarne, a monastery established in the cold and windswept northern county Northumberland, and this wild place would have felt like home to him. Even today there is a long walk from the nearest road to reach the chapel, but this is part of its charm. Little is left inside the chapel to tell of its extraordinary 1,400-year life, but the fact that it was emptied and used as a barn for centuries is the only reason it survived at all. It is open all the time.

SECRETS

While you're there

BRADWELL is a very pretty village with a tiny Georgian lock-up (a single-roomed overnight prison) and an interesting church – St Thomas's – with an 18th-century brick tower.

Secret place to stay

THE GREEN MAN, Bradwell (greenmanbradwellonsea.co.uk). An unspoilt 16th-century inn on the river Blackwater catering for families as well as foodies.

Mottisfont Abbey

HAMPSHIRE

Mottisfont is a ruined monastery that like so many, has gained a romantic air. A spring that fed the river Test here gave the abbey its name ('font' in the abbey's name means 'spring'). Established in the 13th century by a wealthy businessman and courtier, the religious community that lived here suffered at the hands of the plague and never recovered. At the dissolution in 1539 Henry VIII gave Mottisfont to his friend the Lord Chamberlain, William Sandys, in exchange for the villages of Chelsea and Paddington. Bizarrely the residential parts

SECRETS

MOTTISFONT ABBEY, Mottisfont, nr Romsey, Hampshire, SO51 0LP (nationaltrust.org.uk). ☎ 01794 340757. Open: House Feb–Oct 11.00–17.00. Garden open most of the year 10.00–17.00; check website for details. Price: adult £8.10, child £4.05, family £19.80.

While you're there

Visit the small town of **ROMSEY** with its delightful ancient houses and walks along the river Test.

Secret place to stay

THE WHITE HORSE, Romsey (thewhitehorseromsey.co.uk). Offers a home from home.

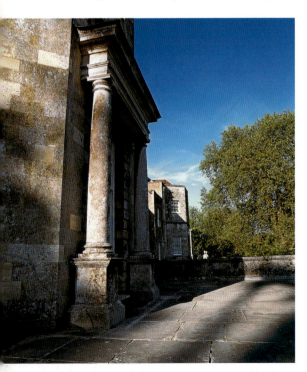

of the monastery were demolished and the church nave and tower were converted into Sandy's new house.

Inside Mottisfont Abbey, the maginificent drawing room mural by Rex Whistler (1905–44) is a superb example of trompe l'oeil. Whistler's subject – this was his last work – is a sort of Gothic extravaganza of pillars and pelmets, which was commissioned when the house was occupied from the 1930s by Maud Gilbert, a partron of the arts.

Another of Mottisfont's delights is that it provides a setting for the National Collection of old-fashioned roses – the sort that look divine and smell like heaven – in gardens that also include mature trees (including the biggest plane tree in the country) and splendid lawns running down to the river Test.

The classical splendours of Mottisfont Abbey.

Gardens of the Rose HERTFORDSHIRE

Tucked away in this pretty corner of Hertfordshire is the most extraordinary collection of roses – here among some 30,000 varieties you will find old varieties and new, rare kinds and common.

Run by the Royal National Rose Society, the gardens reveal the English passion for this ubiquitous flower, but they are also filled with what rose fans call companion plants – that is, plants that go well with roses.

Vast beds of roses can be found everywhere: climbers, standard roses, dwarf varieties and much more. Here you will find everything from Seagull to Bobby James, from Summer Wine to Klifsgate. There are broad terraces, small formal gardens, pergolas and arbours – for the rose lover there really is nothing quite like it anywhere else. The Queen Mother Garden includes a huge selection of old-fashioned roses, and there are trial grounds and a peace garden. More than 100 varieties of clematis are also on view and judicious planting means that something spectacular will be blooming from early in the season until late.

The gardens are a riot of colour in summer.

SECRETS

GARDENS OF THE ROSE, Chiswell Green, St. Albans, Hertfordshire, AL2 3NR (rnrs.org.uk). ☎ 01727 850461. Entrance times and prices vary so check website.

While you're there

Visit the **VERULAMIUM MUSEUM** in nearby St Albans (stalbansmuseums.org.uk). This has numerous fascinating Roman artefacts as well as recreated Roman rooms.

Secret place to stay

WHITE HART HOTEL, St Albans (whiteharthotel.org). One of the little known wonders of St Albans, the building is 600 years old and faces the abbey.

The Fighting Cocks

HERTFORDSHIRE

Several public houses have claimed to be the oldest in the country, but a strong contender for the title – and one that is currently accepted by the *Guinness Book of Records* – is the Fighting Cocks in the heart of old St Albans.

The pub sits below the great cathedral, which tends to be the main draw for visitors, so the Fighting Cocks is easily missed. Parts of this picturesque crooked timber building are certainly extremely old – archaeologists have identified elements from the mid-11th century and pretty much every period since.

But the exact history of the Fighting Cocks is difficult to trace. Some experts have said that, despite the fact that this is an 11th-century structure on an 8th-century site, it has not always been a pub. There is some evidence – hotly disputed by others – that the Fighting Cocks was a pigeon house before it became an alehouse in 1485. But whatever the rights and wrongs of the arguments the Fighting Cocks is very old indeed – one of its bars was formerly a cockfighting pit, and it is said that Oliver Cromwell insisted on keeping his horse in the bar while he slept upstairs.

The Fighting Cocks in St Albans.

SECRETS

YE OLD FIGHTING COCKS,
16 Abbey Mill Lane, St Albans, Hertfordshire, AL3 4HE, (yeoldefightingcocks.co.uk).
☎ 01727 869152.

While you're there

Visit **ST STEPHEN'S CHURCH,** which has work from every period back to around 940, tthough is now largely medieval in style. Sympathetic Victorian renovations provide a peaceful ambience.

Secret place to stay

ST MICHAEL'S MANOR HOTEL, St Albans ☎ 01727 864444. (stmichaelsmanor.com). Expensive but beautiful in a lakeside setting.

Welwyn Roman Baths HERTFORDSHIRE

Road builders usually destroy everything in their path but not always – which is why drivers on the A1(M) in Hertfordshire now roar above one of the county's best-kept secrets. Beneath the busy modern roadway, engineers managed to preserve in situ a remarkable Roman bathhouse, built more than 1,700 years ago and once part of a much larger villa complex.

Evidence of the Romans' ingenious underfloor heating system survives here, together with the various rooms that provided them with hot baths, tepid baths and freezing plunge pools. You can still see where slaves would have sat, working

The Roman baths beneath the A1(M)!

continually to keep the fires stoked that heated the floors and the water.

There are numerous displays showing how Roman life in the area was organized, and the site has been arranged so that visitors can walk from bath to bath, just as the Romans did nearly 2,000 years ago.

Bembridge and Culver Downs

ISLE OF WIGHT

Bembridge and Culver Downs give you the sense of being on top of the world as you gaze across the Solent (provided the weather is clear!) towards Portsmouth and the North Downs beyond. Compared to the tea shops and tourist towns that attract many to the island, the downs are relatively little visited – a pity given the fabulous sense of space and air they provide. The Victorian Poet Laureate Alfred, Lord Tennyson, who loved these downs and lived nearby for many years, thought this the best air in the world. It was, he said, 'like champagne'.

If you walk the 8km (5 miles) from Bembridge to Sandown via Bembridge Down and Culver Cliffs you'll see all that this spectacular part of the country has to offer.

View across the downs to the Solent.

Bembridge and Culver Downs are owned by the National Trust and form a spectacular chalk headland at the north end of Sandown Bay.

High on Culver Down is the Napoleonic Bembridge Fort, also owned by the National Trust. At Bembridge itself there is a tiny ancient church – one of the smallest in the country, as well as the island's last remaining windmill. Built in 1700 but only recently restored, the windmill has most of its original wooden gear. The Shipwreck and Maritime Museum, also at Bembridge, has a fascinating collection of artefacts including a 70-year-old jar of rum salvaged from a wreck.

SECRETS

While you're there

Visit **BLACKGANG CHINE**, a remarkable deep, narrow gorge that boasts unique flora.

Secret place to stay

BOURNE HALL COUNTRY HOTEL, Shanklin (bournehallhotel.co.uk). Beautifully situated and reasonably priced.

St Augustine's Church KENT

With its strange tower, St Augustine's Church lies at the heart of the small, neatly ordered village of Brookland in Walland Marsh. The nearest big town is Tenterden some 20km (12 miles) to the north. The most immediately striking thing about this unusual church is that its bell tower is detached from the church. It is also octagonal, with a conical timber roof, and is certainly contemporary with the rest of the 13th-century structure.

The church itself will make you feel decidedly wobbly when you reach the nave, for the whole of this part of the building – notice particularly the nave arches – leans out at an impossible angle (caused by subsidence). 'Why,' the visitor invariably asks, 'has the church not collapsed?' As in the case of the Leaning Tower of Pisa, the answer is that no one really knows. But the fact that the church has not collapsed, and is

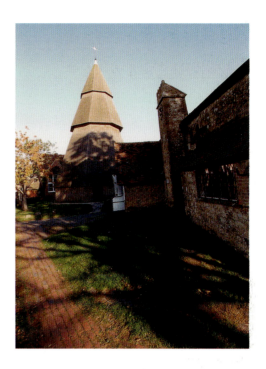

The crazy-angled 13th-century bell tower.

apparently in no danger of doing so, should be celebrated, for there is much to enjoy in this one building.

On the south wall there is a splendid painting of the greatest of the Kentish martyrs – St Thomas Becket – and the nave is that rare thing, a survivor of the Victorian mania for 'improving' ancient churches. St Augustine's also retains its beautiful Georgian box pews and pulpit. And if this isn't enough, this little-known church has a lead font that is arguably the most unusual anywhere in Britain. Almost certainly Norman, the font shows the signs of the zodiac together with their accompanying symbols – there is nothing quite like it anywhere else and its exact significance and origins are unknown.

Derek Jarman's Garden KENT

Best known as an artist and film maker, Derek Jarman (1942–94) came to this remote, some would say bleak, corner of Kent during the last years of his life. Round his tiny cottage, which faces out across the vast sea of stones toward the huge futuristic power station, he created a remarkable contemporary garden.

If you decide to visit, you must divest your mind of the normal conceptions of gardens and gardening, for Derek Jarman created his patch of green from objects picked up on the beach, and the resulting garden is all the more interesting as a result. More like a sculpture or installation art, the garden mixes found objects with stones and a few salt-tolerant plants.

SECRETS

DEREK JARMAN'S GARDEN, Prospect Cottage, Dungeness, Kent.

While you're there
Ride on the wonderful narrow gauge **ROMNEY HYTHE AND DYMCHURCH RAILWAY,** across unspoilt marshlands (rhdr.org.uk).

Secret place to stay
GEORGE HOTEL, Lydd.
(thegeorgelydd.com). A real gem.

Derek Jarman used beach finds and his imagination to create a unique garden in a hostile environment. The garden can be viewed from a single-track road that passes close by the property, though walking will allow a better appreciation of the spirit of the place. The house is privately occupied.

The Grand Shaft

KENT

Three clockwise staircases, one above the other, rise up from Dover's Snargate Street through an 8m (26ft)-diameter shaft cut through the cliffs to the Western Heights, the clifftop defences built to protect England against invasion during the Napoleonic Wars.

Hidden from view, the Grand Shaft – as the triple staircase is known – was built to allow troops to get from town to the defences as quickly as possible. Before it was built, the soldiers had to clamber down steep, chalky trackways that were treacherous during bad weather.

The Grand Shaft was the brainchild of Brigadier General Twiss. He suggested it in 1804 and by 1809 it was complete. Brick-lined, with an occasional window for light and with steps made at great expense from Purbeck limestone, it rises some 43m (140 ft). It has three staircases, and because the class structure of England was so rigid in the Victorian period each staircase was designated for the use of a different rank of soldier. One staircase was for officers and their ladies, another for sergeants and their wives and the third for soldiers and their women. All three staircases met at a short sloping stretch at the bottom of the tunnel that led down to the barred entrance in Snargate Street.

Snargate Street dates back to the 15th century – then it was actually on the beach – and the cliffs round about are still riddled with tunnels, old storehouses and hidden cellars.

A view up the Grand Shaft.

SECRETS

GRAND SHAFT AND WESTERN HEIGHTS
South Military Road, Dover
(doverwesternheights.org). ☎ 01304
201200. Open in summer; phone for details.

While you're there

Visit the **ROMAN LIGHTHOUSE** next to Dover Castle, one of the few remaining almost complete Roman buildings in Britain.

Secret place to stay

WALLETT'S COURT, Westcliffe
(wallettscourthotelspa.com). Ten minutes' drive from Dover, this ancient country house has a superb restaurant.

St Leonard's Church KENT

The wall paintings and over-filled graveyards are long gone; and the dark, dusty corners of our oldest-surviving churches have been swept clean, whitewashed and made suitable for coffee mornings. But one or two churches hidden away in obscure parts of the country retain something of their dark pre-Reformation past. One such is St Leonard's Church in Hythe, where thousands of human bones are still stored – as medieval churches would have stored them – in a charnel house.

However, it is probably fair to say that most churches had their charnel houses in the churchyard; some kept the bones in an odd, unused chapel. At St Leonard's the charnel house was and is under the chancel in the crypt, although even calling it a crypt is odd, as a crypt would normally allow entrance to the main body of the church and this does not. The likely explanation is that the St Leonard's crypt is an ambulatory – a consecrated route for processions of one kind or another.

Today, the crypt, or ambulatory, houses more than 8,000 thigh bones and 2,000 skulls – all have been dated to the early Middle Ages and have survived because conditions in the crypt are – quite by chance – ideal for the bones' preservation. When you've seen the bones, take time to explore the rest of the church, which is equally fascinating. The archway to St Edmund's chapel is clearly Saxon, but the Normans added a nave in 1080 and the aisles were added early in the 12th century.

Neatly stacked skulls greet visitors to the crypt.

SECRETS

While you're there

Enjoy the ancient unspoilt little town of **HYTHE**, which retains its ancient street plan.

THE AMERICAN GARDEN in Smallwood, nearby, will delight gardeners. This tranquil space is a haven in springtime.

Secret place to stay

THE SWAN HOTEL, Hythe (theswanhotelhythe.co.uk). Offers reasonable rates in a refurbished coaching inn.

Eastbury Manor House LONDON

The Elizabethan Eastbury Manor House in Barking.

Hidden away in the seemingly endless suburban streets of the London borough of Barking is a remarkable survival. Eastbury Manor House is an almost unaltered Elizabethan merchant's house that no visitor to London should miss. The house was built in the 1550s (analysis of the roof timbers have confirmed this) and the red-brick frontage and glorious elaborate chimney stacks still look just as they would have done almost five centuries ago, although the interior is largely altered.

Wall paintings in the Great Chamber include fishing scenes, and there is a wonderful original spiral oak staircase built in its own turret. Exposed timbers can be viewed in the attic and there is a delightful cobbled courtyard, as well as a small garden.

SECRETS

EASTBURY MANOR HOUSE, Eastbury Square, Barking, London, IG11 9SN (nationaltrust.org.uk). ☎ 0208 724 1002. Open: Jan–Dec Mon, Tues, 1st and 2nd Sat of month 10.00–16.00. Price: adult £3, child £1, family £6.

While you're there

RAINHAM HALL, Havering, is a stunningly picturesque Georgian house filled with fine early joinery and other features (nationaltrust.org.uk).

Secret place to stay

THE WEST HAM UNITED HOTEL (westhamhotel.co.uk). Football fans will be fascinated to hear that they can stay in a hotel within West Ham football ground.

Boston Manor House LONDON

West London was largely rural until the end of World War I. The river Thames provided a good route into London, even in winter when the roads were muddy. Mansions, palaces and gentlemen's houses sprang up in and around the villages lying along the road from London to Bath – a road that took in villages such as Acton, Brentford, Isleworth and Hounslow. Despite the fact that these once unspoilt villages have been altered beyond all recognition by population growth and urban development, an occasional gem from the past still survives.

One of the loveliest of these gems is Boston Manor House, which dates from 1623 and sits in its own grounds. It was built for Lady Marty Reade, whose initials are still to be seen in the drawing room ceiling. Highlights of the property tour include the magnificent decorated plaster ceilings in the state rooms, and the carved Jacobean fireplace, which depicts scenes that include the angel Gabriel telling Abraham not to sacrifice Isaac. The Boston Manor gardens, with their ornamental lake, are also well worth a visit.

SECRETS

BOSTON MANOR HOUSE, 69–75 Boston Manor Road, Brentford, Middlesex, TW8 9JJ (hounslow.info/arts/bostonmanorhouse/index.htm). ☎ 0845 456 2800. The state rooms and dining room are open April–Oct, Sat, Sun & BH 14.30–17.00.

While you're there

Visit OSTERLEY MANOR HOUSE and grounds. The magnificent red-brick house is well known, but the working farm, lake and extensive wild grounds less so (nationaltrust.org.uk).

Secret place to stay

HOBART HALL HOTEL, Richmond (hobarthall.net). A must!

Seventeenth-century Boston Manor House still has its own grounds.

The Dove

LONDON

The old village of Hammersmith in West London almost vanished during the 1960s when comprehensive redevelopment pushed a six-lane highway through this quiet riverside community, but a small part survives, and down a tiny alleyway at its heart can be found one of London's most delightful inns.

The Dove, which was built toward the end of the 17th century, can only be reached on foot – the best way is along the riverside path from Hammersmith Bridge – and on each side of its little alleyway are tall 18th-century houses.

There is a tiny snug bar with room for only half a dozen drinkers and a slightly larger public bar where, until the 1980s, a real fire was kept blazing. At the back, a small garden overlooks the river. It was in this little house

The Dove is a snug hideaway in winter.

SECRETS

THE DOVE, 19 Upper Mall, Hammersmith, London, W6 9TA (fullers.co.uk).
☎ 0208 748 9474.

While you're there

Visit **BRADMORE HOUSE** at Hammersmith Broadway. Only the façade of this fine baroque house remains (with offices behind), but this architecturally acclaimed house was once the country home of actress Anne Oldfield (1683–1730).

Secret place to stay

HAZLITT'S HOTEL (hazlittshotel.com/hazlitts/) Hop on the Underground to Leicester Square and you can stay in 18th-century splendour.

that the 18th-century poet James Thompson wrote his celebrated work *The Seasons,* and for 300 years, until the trade vanished early in the 20th century, this was a favourite haunt of Thames watermen.

Trafalgar Square Lock-up LONDON

At one time most English towns and villages had lock-ups – small, single-celled buildings where local drunks might be kept secure for the night, or where thieves or other antisocial individuals could be kept to await the arrival of the magistrate. At the south-east corner of Trafalgar Square and missed by almost every tourist who comes, there is a lock-up that is unique – even by the standards of these odd little prisons – because it is also Britain's (and possibly the world's) smallest police station.

The structure looks like a rather fat lamp post and it is only when you look closely that you notice the tiny door and window. There is barely room for two people to stand upright inside, but it is said that this tiny lock-up had – and still has – a direct telephone link to

It is easy to miss this lock-up.

Scotland Yard. The Trafalgar Square Lock-up was still in use in an official capacity right up to the 1960s.

SECRETS

While you're there

Take a close look at the capital at the top of the **COLUMN** on which Nelson's statue stands and the bronze bas-reliefs at the bottom of the column showing Nelson's victories (as well as his yet more famous death). All are made from French cannons captured after the Battle of Trafalgar.

Secret place to stay

BROWN'S HOTEL (brownshotel.com). Few people realize that London's oldest hotel – the very first to open in the capital – is in the heart of Mayfair. It's expensive but rather special.

Linley Sambourne House LONDON

What an extraordinary house this is. Great houses and churches often survive intact, but the interiors of the houses of the middle and working classes tend to vanish without trace. Linley Sambourne house, named after the cartoonist who lived here from 1874 to 1910, is a perfect example of a well-to-do but by no means aristocratic household of the mid-Victorian period.

When Sambourne and his young wife moved into the house, which had only been built four years earlier, they decorated it in the fashionable aesthetic style – characterized by heavy velvet drapes, William Morris wallpapers, ornate Turkey carpets, and a vast clutter of china ornaments.

Sambourne earned his living as a cartoonist, mostly for *Punch*, for almost half a century. Most of his drawings were completed in this house and numerous examples of his work can be seen, along with his photographs – like many artists of the time he was fascinated by this still relatively new art form.

The house remained substantially unchanged through the 20th century through sheer luck. The Sambourne's son Roy inherited the house and did little to it, probably because he never married. When he in turn died, he left the house to his elder sister Maud. She was passionate about preserving it intact, largely because – as she said herself – she'd been so happy there as a child. Her daughter Anne proposed that she and her friends, including the Poet Laureate Sir John Betjeman, should found a Victorian Society to preserve the house and its contents.

SECRETS

LINLEY SAMBOURNE HOUSE,
18 Stafford Terrace, London, W8 7BH
☎ 0207 602 3316 (to book tours).
Guided tours only at various times
throughout the day. Price: adult £6, child £1.

While you're there

Just a few minutes away is the **HOUSE** once
owned by artist Sir Frederick Leighton.
Don't miss the wonderful Islamic room
(rbkc.gov.uk/subsites/museums/leighton
housemuseum.aspx).

Secret place to stay

THE GATE HOTEL (gatehotel.co.uk). This
delightful little 19th-century house is hidden
away at the top end of Portobello Road.

Geffrye Museum

LONDON

With its jaded air of past commercial prosperity, Kingsland Road in London's East End is an unlikely setting for a row of exquisite 18th-century almshouses. The Geffrye almshouses, which were built by Sir Robert Geffrye for the Ironmongers' Company in 1715, now house one of the most interesting exhibitions in the country.

Here, well away from the main tourist areas of the city, you will find a remarkable collection of English furniture, pictures and other fittings in a series of chronologically arranged period rooms.

This is time travel on foot, as a tour of the museum takes you through typical rooms of every period from the early 17th century to the 1960s and beyond. Here you will find the dark, beautiful, early oak furniture and panelling of the Elizabethans, the light and elegance of a Georgian sitting room, heavy Victorian interior, and 1950s room filled with utility furniture and an early television. The best thing about the museum is that the interiors reflect in many instances the life of the less well off and the attention to detail is remarkable.

Georgian interior at Geffrye Museum.

SECRETS

GEFFRYE MUSEUM, 136 Kingsland Road, Shoreditch, London E2 8EA (geffrye-museum.org.uk).
Open: Tues–Sat 10.00–17.00, Sun & BH Mon 12.00–17.00. Free admission.

While you're there

Nip on the Tube to Green Park and visit the **QUEEN'S CHAPEL** near St James's Palace. Built by Inigo Jones at the beginning of the 17th century it is hugely important, yet often overlooked (www.royal.gov.uk).

Secret place to stay

THE GEORGIAN HOUSE HOTEL. Westminster (georgianhousehotel.co.uk).
A bed and breakfast hotel located in the centre of London. Built in 1851, it is still run by descendants of the original family.

Catherine of Aragon's House

LONDON

This is a tall, narrow house at 49 Bankside, Cardinal's Wharf – once part of a terrace – that overlooks the Thames on the south bank of the river opposite St Paul's Cathedral. It is the last of the many bankside houses that once lined the river.

When Henry VIII's wife Catherine (1485–1536) arrived from Spain she is said to have stayed here, and two centuries later, when Christopher Wren was building St Paul's, he too is said to have stayed in the house to supervise the work on his great cathedral. The house has now been dated to 1710 so neither of these claims can be true, although they may have inadvertently helped preserve the house from demolition. The house is privately owned.

Catherine of Aragon once stayed here.

SECRETS

While you're there

Don't miss the tiny alleyway at the side of the old house. This is **CARDINAL'S CAP ALLEY**, the narrowest road in London.

Secret place to stay

MAD HATTER HOTEL
☎ 0207 401 9222.
A delightfully named listed Victorian building.

SECRETS

DENIS SEVERS' HOUSE
18 Folgate Street, Spitalfields, London, E1 6BX
(dennissevershouse.co.uk).
Opening times and prices vary so check the website.
No children.

While you're there

Visit nearby **SPITALFIELDS CHURCH**, the masterpiece of Nicholas Hawksmoor, who rebuilt many of London's churches after the Great Fire.

Secret place to eat

FAZENDA. 13 Leyden Street, Spitalfields, London, E1 7LE
☎ 0207 375 0577. Authentic Italian; reasonable prices.

Dennis Severs' House LONDON

This strange little house is in Spitalfields, one of the most unspoilt areas of early 18th-century London. Here a grid of streets retains their magnificent door cases and much of their interior fireplaces and panelling. They are known as silk weavers' houses because they were built by immigrant silk weavers, who settled in London to escape persecution in France. Typically the attics of the houses were organized to fit their silk looms.

Most of the houses are still privately owned, but one can be visited. It was formerly lived in by Denis Severs (1948–99), an American with a passion for all things English. When he retired to the house he wanted it to appear as if an 18th-century family was still living there. To achieve this, there is no electric light, the rooms are left cluttered and dusty, in some rooms the plaster is crumbling and on a dining table can usually be seen what looks like the remains of a half-finished meal. To preserve the atmosphere, visitors are not allowed to talk while visiting the house.

Visiting Dennis Severs' House feels like time travelling to an 18th-century home where inhabitants have just gone to bed.

The George Inn

LONDON

The George Inn in Southwark is London's last representative of a style of building that was common throughout the long centuries when all transport was by horse. In former times there were at least half a dozen galleried inns in London. They were built around a courtyard and the rooms on each level gave onto a walkway or gallery. It is a style of building that would have been familiar to Shakespeare and his contemporaries. The courtyard enabled coaches to enter and be unloaded in the midst as it were of the inn space. On the ground floor would have been the public rooms for drinking and eating, and above, entered via the external galleries, would have been the bedrooms.

The oldest of the George's bars still has its 18th-century interior – with tavern clock, crooked timber floors, two fireplaces and benches built into the walls. It is without question a Southwark scene from at least two centuries ago. Only one side of what would have originally been a four-sided inn still exists, but when you look up from the courtyard you can at least be sure that this is an authentic view into London's past – a past that Dickens and Shakespeare would have recognized. Dickens even mentions The George by name in *Little Dorrit*.

There had been an inn on the site of the George since the 14th century, but the present building dates from just after a huge fire, which destroyed most of Southwark in 1676.

Southwark's ancient coaching inn, The George.

SECRETS

THE GEORGE INN, The George Inn Yard, 77 Borough High Street, Southwark, London, SE1 1NH ☎ 0207 407 2056.

While you're there

Nip along the river to Lambeth and visit the **TRADESCANT GARDEN MUSEUM**, now housed in a redundant church next to Lambeth Palace (gardenmuseum.org.uk).

Secret place to stay

WINDMILL ON THE COMMON, Clapham (windmillclapham.co.uk). A wonderful 18th-century building, carefully converted.

Berry Bros & Rudd and Lock & Co.

LONDON

Berry Bros & Rudd began trading from their shop in St James's Street at the end of the 17th century, and when you step inside you realize that very little has changed in terms of decoration, fixtures and fittings in the intervening 300 years. Ancient floors and benches slope in all directions and the walls are crooked, which befits a house that is much older than it looks.

Byron bought his wine here, as did Peel, the Duke of Wellington, Laurence Olivier and Evelyn Waugh. The business is still family owned and run. At one side of the shop

Lock & Co. have traded here since 1764.

is an ancient lane that leads to a tiny secluded courtyard – London was once a dense network of tiny lanes and courts such as this, and this is one of the last remaining.

Lock & Co., just a few doors down from Berry Bros, has been making hats in London since the 17th century. Since 1764 they've been in this shop. Locks have made hats for everyone from Nelson to Charlie Chaplin. Most famously they invented the bowler hat, which was, until the 1960s, the universal headgear of male office workers in the City of London. The bowler hat actually started life as a gamekeeper's hat – it was designed for the immensely wealthy Lord Coke of Norfolk, whose gamekeepers were occasionally attacked by poachers – the bowler was, it seems, an early form of crash helmet! How it made the transition to the square mile is still a mystery.

SECRETS

BERRY BROS & RUDD, 3 St James's Street, London, SW1A 1EF (www.bbr.com).

LOCK & CO., 6 St. James's Street, London, SW1A 1EF (lockhatters.co.uk).

While you're there

Go into St James's Park, where you can gaze at the last grand London mansion still owned by the family that built it. The ancestors of Diana, Princess of Wales built **SPENCER HOUSE** in the 1750s (spencerhouse.co.uk).

Secret place to stay

BEAUFORT HOTEL (thebeaufort.rtrk.co.uk). This small, privately owned hotel isn't cheap but has a great reputation.

Kensal Green Cemetery LONDON

Most visitors brave enough to include a cemetery on their London itinerary go to Highgate Cemetery to the north of the city, but tucked away by the side of the Grand Union Canal over to the west in what was, until recently, a fairly poor part of North Kensington, Kensal Green Cemetery is an extraordinary and little-known monument to Victorian funeral piety.

Until the coming of the canal in the 18th century this was a quiet place: there were a few houses at the junction of Harrow Road and Kilburn Lane, but the rest was open farmland, with an odd isolated inn, and London was a day's walk away. But by the early 1800s, the small

One of Kensal Green's elaborate tombs.

SECRETS

KENSAL GREEN CEMETERY
(kensalgreencemetery.com).
Open: Apr–Sept Mon–Sat 9.00–18.00, Sun 10.00–18.00; Oct–Mar Mon–Sat 9.00–17.00, Sun 10.00–17.00; Bank Holidays 10.00–13.00.

While you're there

Enjoy a walk along the nearby **GRAND UNION CANAL**, one of Britain's first industrial waterways.

Secret place to stay

TUDOR LODGE HOTEL, Pinner (thetudorlodge.net). This former farmhouse dates back to the early 16th century.

village, centred around the junction and its green, was expanding. By the 1830s London's church graveyards were filled to bursting and All Soul's Cemetery (the land was owned by All Souls College, Oxford) was opened in 1832 to ease the problem. Within a few years Kensal Green Cemetery, as it quickly became known, was the fashionable place to be buried. Planned with vistas and planted with trees and shrubs, the cemetery became the final resting place for London's burgeoning population.

Among the extraordinary monuments, the cemetery contains Greek temples, Egyptian halls, gothic fantasies and medieval castles, as well as more ordinary but equally fascinating gravestones and tombs. Among the tombs to look out for are those of Sir Anthony Panizzi, who created the famous reading room at the British Museum; Charles Babbage, who created the first computer; authors Wilkie Collins, William Makepeace Thackeray and Anthony Trollope, as well as the great Victorian engineer – Isambard Kingdom Brunel.

London Wetland Centre LONDON

Who would believe this scene was in London?

There is nothing quite like this anywhere else in the world. In the heart of one of the world's biggest cities, is a wildlife reserve that covers more than 42ha (105 acres). The mixture of habitats created from these disused waterworks – the reservoirs once supplied Londoners with clean water – include grassland, mudflat, reed beds and open lakes.

Paths take you through and around this wild and very natural-looking place, which has attracted a host of rare and not so rare species of duck, geese and waders. There are hides, and visitors are presented with binoculars for the duration of their tour. Species you might be lucky enough to see – depending on the time of year – include grebe, cormorant, heron, kingfisher, tern, wigeon, mallard, coot and tufted duck. There are more than 30 ponds and lakes, nearly 5km (3 miles) of walkways, 27,000 trees and more than 200,000 aquatic plants. Children are given little nets and allowed to fish for larvae and water insects, which staff then explain to them.

SECRETS

WWT LONDON WETLAND CENTRE
Queen Elizabeth's Walk, Barnes, London, SW13 9WT (wwt.org.uk/visit-us/london). ☎ 0208 409 4401. Open: Summer (until end Oct) 9.30–18.00; winter (from Nov) 9.30–17.00. Price: adult £10.99, child: £6.10, family: £30.60.

While you're there

WALK half a mile towards Hammersmith along the Barnes side of the river Thames. It's like stepping into deep countryside and few bother to walk it.

Secret place to stay

QUINN'S HOTEL, Richmond (quinnshotel.com). Lovely Georgian house on the edge of Richmond, five minutes' walk from the river.

St Peter and St Paul

NORFOLK

England contains a mass of remarkable hidden churches. They can be found down lost lanes in out-of-the-way places or concealed behind later monolithic developments. But here in Norfolk, between the villages of Reepham and Cawston, in a county blessed with far more than its fair share of memorable churches, is a building that offers a dazzling mass of medieval craftsmanship.

Wherever you look there are carvings in 15th-century stonework – dragons and monkeys can be found on the misericords (a ledge on which the clergy perched) beneath the oak choir seats, along with flowers, bunches of grapes and swans. Why the medieval craftsmen made these images in a place they would rarely be seen (beneath the tip-up seats) remains a mystery, but it may be connected with the medieval idea of the bestiary. Whatever strange creature man could imagine or create was somehow seen as a further testament to the glory of God.

The armrests at St Peter and St Paul are especially beautiful with their strange carved creatures – monkeys and dragons predominate, but with strange additions, such as webbed feet, for example. High above, the ancient timber roof is equally profusely carved – here (if you have sharp eyes) you will see numerous wooden angels and beautifully carved bosses. Bizarrely, given that churches are supposed to be welcoming, the doors to the church are guarded on either side by fierce-looking creatures carrying heavy clubs. They are known as wodewoses and echo older pagan creatures.

The church contains medieval masterpieces.

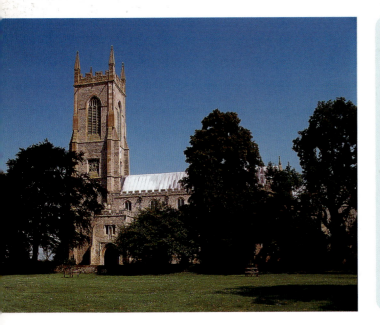

Little Walsingham

NORFOLK

Walsingham has been a place of pilgrimage for Catholics since the Middle Ages, ever since a noblewoman built a shrine to the Virgin Mary following a vision. Today, it is more popular than ever as a place for the religious to visit. The village, too, has much of interest for the general visitor.

Despite the fact that little of medieval Walsingham remains, the place has a curiously ancient feel to it. The ruins of two ancient religious houses are here, both destroyed by the hand of Henry VIII. There's something almost eccentric about it, too – the railway station, for example, has an onion dome on its roof. The dome was the work of a Russian Orthodox monk, who came here in the 1960s and sought permission to turn the disused building into a chapel.

You have to leave Walsingham to find a truly ancient place, but if you make the journey to the Slipper Chapel in Houghton

Walsingham has many unusual and attractive features to delight the visitor.

St Giles you will be doing just as medieval pilgrims would have done. The chapel, which is largely 14th century, gets its name from the fact that pilgrims to Walsingham would stop here before tackling the last mile or so of their journey, and they would remove their shoes so it could be completed in a suitably pious (and painful!) condition.

SECRETS

While you're there

Just up the road on the north Norfolk coast is the pretty village of **BLAKENEY**, which leads on to the wild bird-rich sands and sea. Delicious crab sandwiches are always available from a hut near the beach.

Secret place to stay

BLAKENEY HOTEL, Blakeney (blakeney-hotel.co.uk). Quayside position with views across the estuary.

Blakeney Point

NORFOLK

The whole of the Norfolk coast might justly be termed a bird sanctuary, for wherever you go the marshes and creeks, the sands and inlets are filled with birds of all species. But Blakeney Point, lonely and remote though it might be, is truly special. It's a simple shingle spit 5.75km (3½ miles) long, but that narrow space is one of the great secrets of Norfolk, for this bleak promontory has been thrown up, created as it were, from nothing by centuries of wave action.

You can take a ferry to the point itself, but it's more fun – and far more bracing – to walk out along the narrow windswept spit; with a big sea running and the wind up, it is a most exhilarating experience. At the point itself the sea has created a wider place of sand and shingle, and it is here that huge numbers of migrating birds make their first landfall.

In addition to birds the point is also hugely popular with seals, which rest on the pebbles amid the thousands of geese and ducks. The point is also a major site for nesting terns and for twitchers, those fanatical birdwatchers who will travel any distance to spot and then list a rare migrant.

The coast is popular with sailors and day visitors, as well as birds.

Welney Wildfowl Reserve NORFOLK

Welney was once the centre of a wildfowl-hunting culture that dated back to the arrival of humankind in this flooded, forbidding corner of England. Early settlers lived by duck and goose, as a local saying has it, particularly in winter when the meres were frozen and a little money could be raised by bringing captured geese and ducks to market for sale.

Even into the early part of the 20th century, puntgunners worked the marshes here – lying face down in their flat canoes they would drift within range of a raft of teal

Vast numbers of wildfowl visit Welney, especially in the winter.

SECRETS

WWT WELNEY WETLAND CENTRE
Hundred Foot Bank, Welney, nr Wisbech, PE14 9TN (wwt.org.uk/visit-us/welney). ☎ 01353 863524. Open: end Feb–Oct 9.30–17.00; Nov–Feb Mon, Tues & Wed 10.00–17.00, Thurs–Sun 10.00–20.00. Price: adult £6.64, child £3.27, family £17.23.

While you're there

Visit nearby **KING'S LYNN**. Few tourists bother to visit this ancient place, but it has streets of lovely old houses and a delightful atmosphere.

Secret place to stay

OLD RECTORY, King's Lynn (theoldrectory-kingslynn.com). Definitely the place to stay.

or tufted duck before firing their huge blunderbuss-like guns at the vast flocks of birds. The shrapnell was guaranteed to hit numbers, and the catch was quickly collected in nets.

Today, Welney, the strip of the Washes between the Old and New Bedford rivers that floods every winter, is still an extraordinarily rich place for waders and wildfowl, and indeed for those who come to watch and study, rather than shoot, them. Winter is the best time to visit when the hordes of migrating birds escape the worst of the Arctic winter and arrive here in their tens of thousands – the list of species you are likely to see is almost endless: among the duck there are pintail, shoveller, pochard, wigeon and teal, but there are also geese, including pinkfoot and greylag, grebes and Bewick swans.

Blickling Hall

NORFOLK

Blickling Hall is an impressive country estate, incorporating a splendid multi-gabled house that is a classic example of Jacobean architecture. For all its size, it does not have the imposing grandeur of, say, Hatfield or Burghley – perhaps because it was always too far from London for its owner to wield great political influence. Instead, it has an almost homely air.

The hall was famed, in earlier times, as the residence of the Boleyn family and it is reputed that Anne Boleyn, the second wife of Henry VIII, was born here, though to be exact, the current house dates from a later time and was rebuilt on the ruins of the old hall in the 17th century.

Blickling Hall is multi-gabled and imposing.

SECRETS

BLICKLING ESTATE, Blickling, Norwich, Norfolk, NR11 6NF (nationaltrust.org.uk). ☎ 01263 738030. Ticket prices and opening times vary so check the website.

While you're there

Don't miss the National Trust's **FELBRIGG HALL,** a small gem of a 17th-century house, which includes, in one room, original 18th-century wallpaper. The extensive gardens are wildlife rich and a delight to walk in.

Secret place to stay

BLACK BOYS HOTEL, Aylsham (blackboyshotel.co.uk). Georgian hotel just a short drive from Blickling.

Hidden away inside the house is a most spectacular plaster ceiling, that is well worth seeing. It runs the whole length of the long gallery – almost 40m (130ft) in all. The ceiling is covered with allegorical figures, together with representations of the five senses, plus flowers and swirls of almost dazzling intricacy, and it is surely one of the most spectacular in England.

Blickling is also rightly famed for its Chinese bedroom in which the walls are still covered with the hand-painted Chinese wallpaper first hung in the 18th century. A notable collection of books in the library completes the list of the items that it is essential to see. Outside an impressive ancient yew hedge lines the way to the front of the house. The gardens, which have been redesigned over the centuries according to the latest fashion are a garden lover's paradise.

Stonor Park

OXFORDSHIRE

The Camoys family have lived at Stonor Park for 800 years. Surrounded by the last remnants of what was once a great estate, this ancient house is easy to miss, as it lies off the tourist track, which runs up the Thames and concentrates, in this area, on Henley.

Stonor has an interesting history. The house has medieval, Tudor and Georgian architectural features, a walled garden, private chapel and – nearby – an ancient stone circle, evidence that this quiet valley has been inhabited for thousands of years.

When the Camoys arrived in the 13th century Christianity was still one faith united under the Pope. When Henry VIII decided he wanted a divorce and established a new religion to facilitate it, the Catholic Church and its institutions were systematically destroyed. The Camoys family refused to give up the old faith, despite centuries of persecution. Their lands were sold off bit by bit to pay fines that were levied on Catholics.

Today the house still has that off-the-beaten-track air that enabled the Camoys to survive into a new period of toleration. The house has many connections with great figures of the past – the Catholic martyr Thomas Campion, for example, hid in a concealed room in the attic here. The interior of the house now bears the imprint of 18th-century gothic taste but the Georgian decoration conceals a far older fabric. Perhaps the most unusual thing about the house is that mass has been celebrated here in the chapel continuously since 1349, a record unmatched anywhere else in the country.

SECRETS

STONOR PARK, Henley-on-Thames, Oxfordshire, RG9 6HF (stonor.com). ☎ 01491 638587. Open: House Sun 14.00–17.30, Jul & Aug Sun, Wed 14.00–17.30. Gardens and Chapel 13.00–17.30. Price: House, Gardens, Chapel: adult £8, child £4. Gardens: adult: £4, child £2.

While you're there

Just 5km (3 miles) away is the village of TURVILLE. Tiny, unspoilt and hidden in a dip in the Chiltern Hills.

Secret place to stay

THE OLDE BELL, Henley (theoldebell.co.uk). Dating back to 1100, this old coaching inn is justly famous for using local ingredients in its restaurant.

Stonor Park seems remote despite its location.

Swalcliffe Barn

OXFORDSHIRE

There is just a handful remaining of those amazing cathedral-like barns erected at the end of the Middle Ages to store enough grain for their local communities. One of the very best, and least known, is Swalcliffe Barn near Banbury. This great tithe barn was built for New College Oxford by craftsmen with outstanding skill.

What makes Swalcliffe special is that the vast bulk of its wonderful half-cruck oak timber roof is intact and substantially unaltered since it was first put up. The barn measures 29m (128ft) long by 7m ($22^3/_4$ft) wide. Its walls are 1m (3ft) thick with nine huge half-cruck timbers supporting a roof that weighs more than 100 tons.

New College was founded by William of Wykeham and to provide it with enough money he endowed it with the Manor of Swalcliffe – the college owned the manor, which meant that it enjoyed the income the land produced. The decision to build the great barn was taken in 1401 – a decision still recorded in the college's records. Work began in early 1405 – and it took six years to complete. The barn has stood unchanged for six centuries. Today it houses a fascinating collection of historic agricultural vehicles.

Swalcliffe Barn is built mostly of local limestone, with greyer oolitic limestone in places.

SECRETS

SWALCLIFFE BARN, Shipston Road, Swalcliffe, nr Banbury, OX15 5DR (oxfordshire.gov.uk). ☎ 01295 788728. Open: Easter Sunday–Oct Sun & BH Mon 14.00–17.00. Entry is free.

While you're there

Visit picturesque **DEDDINGTON VILLAGE** just a few miles away.

Secret place to stay

RED LION, Adderbury (redlionhotel-adderbury.co.uk). Built in 1606 it still has a complete list of every landlord.

Great Tew

OXFORDSHIRE

This lovely village lies on the edge of the north Oxfordshire uplands. Its cottages and houses are made from golden ironstone, with stone, sometimes thatched, roofs.

In 1086 just 53 householder tenants are recorded. Over the following centuries, as in other villages, houses collapsed and were rebuilt, but by the 18th century development seems largely to have stopped. In the early 19th century Matthew Boulton, the Birmingham manufacturer responsible for bringing steam power to the British mint, bought the estate that included the village. It was he who was responsible for the look of the village today, since he rebuilt many of the cottages or added to those in existence. The secret of the village's timeless appeal is that throughout the 18th and 19th centuries, whenever the houses were repaired or even rebuilt, the established style was copied –

One of the cottages in Great Tew.

whatever the latest house-building fashion happened to be elsewhere it was ignored here in Great Tew. Even datestones were reinstated in new work, which means that any attempt to date many of the houses is now all but impossible. But this is part of the village's enormous charm – this and the fact that there is no modern housing at all. Much of the village was unoccupied for 50 years following the death of Boulton. But, today the rows of cottages with their box hedges and backdrop of large ornamental trees seem the very picture of old England.

SECRETS

While you're there

Visit the **CHURCH OF ST MICHAEL & ALL ANGELS** in New Road, Great Tew. This beautiful building has a wealth of recently discovered medieval wall paintings.

Secret place to stay

DEDDINGTON ARMS HOTEL, Deddington (deddington-arms-hotel.co.uk).
Just 6km (4 miles) away, the hotel was built in the 1500s and boasts period features and modern cooking.

Mapledurham

OXFORDSHIRE

Situated right on the edge of Reading just half a mile or so from acres of undistinguished 1930s semis, Mapledurham is an astonishing time capsule. The lane that leads down from the aforementioned housing ends at the river Thames and the village. An ancient watermill in crumbling mellow red brick still grinds flour on a commercial basis and rows of tiny cottages face across the lane to the big brick mansion that has been lived in by members of the Blount family for more than 500 years.

Mapledurham House was built towards the end of the 16th century. There had been a substantial timber-framed house here for centuries before that, which passed from the Lyndes family to the Blounts in 1490. Almost a century later Sir Michael Blount – a lieutenant at the Tower of London – decided to rebuild, but he had the sense to incorporate parts of the medieval house in his new brick mansion to create what we see today. The Elizabethan house was remodelled in the 1820s and given new interiors, but the H-shaped house still has its tall chimneys (though these have been altered over the years). There's a 17th-century plaster ceiling in the great chamber, a similarly dated staircase and a great deal of splendid Georgian work.

The Blounts were Catholics, whose estate was much reduced over the centuries because they had to raise money to pay fines imposed on all those who were not members of the Church of England.

Mapledurham Mill on the Thames.

SECRETS

MAPLEDURHAM, Mapledurham, Reading, RG4 7TR (mapledurham.co.uk).
☎ 0118 972 3350. Open: House and watermill: Easter–end Sep Sat, Sun & BH. Prices: adult £8.50, child £3.50.

While you're there

The late 15TH-CENTURY WATERMILL is just a stone's throw away at the side of the river Thames.

Secret place to stay

BEECH HOUSE HOTEL, Reading (beechhousehotel.com). A quiet converted Victorian house just 5km (3 miles) away.

Wayland's Smithy

OXFORDSHIRE

Neolithic burial site of Wayland's Smithy.

This Neolithic burial chamber sits high up on the Ridgeway, an ancient 139km (87mile) pathway. Though the burial chamber has perhaps been over-restored, it is still easy to get a glimpse here, on this remote hilltop, of how England looked in the prehistoric age.

Archaeologists believe that two ditches were originally dug to create a mound here. A wooden building was then erected on the mound and at least 14 bodies were placed in the 'crypt'. By BC3,500 the building had gone and the mound had been enlarged more or less to its present size. At one end of the mound a cross-shaped, stone-lined chamber was then created and six standing stones placed at the entrance to the chamber. Archaeologists believe that at least eight bodies were interred here, but any grave goods that may have accompanied them were stolen long ago – probably in Neolithic times. Two of the standing stones are now missing. We have no idea when the tomb acquired its current name – Wayland was the Saxon god of smithing. Legend has it that if you leave a coin and your horse at the mound in the evening you will return in the morning to find the horse shod and the coin gone. The stonework of the tomb lining is of exceptional quality – remarkable when one considers that these stones were placed here more than 3,000 years ago.

SECRETS

WAYLAND'S SMITHY
(english-heritage.org.uk).
Any reasonable time in daylight hours.
Free admission.

While you're there

Wayland's Smithy is just off the ancient **RIDGEWAY** long-distance path, which is clearly signposted. Why not enjoy a few hours on this splendid ancient route?

Secret place to stay

THE MALT SHOVEL, Lambourn (themaltshovel.com). ☎ 01488 73777. Delightful little inn that is the haunt of racing folk.

St Oswald's Church

OXFORDSHIRE

The best way to approach St Oswald's Church in the village of Widford is via the town of Burford. This beautiful Cotswold town, with ancient golden-stone houses climbing the hillside, is actually just inside Oxfordshire, but it is so typical of the Cotswolds that it's hard to believe that it is not officially in Gloucestershire. Halfway down Burfold's steep hill a narrow right turn is signposted to Widford and Swinford.

Well before Swinford the sharp-eyed visitor may spot, in an apparently empty field away to the left, and on a slope above the river Windrush, a small, rather lonely-looking chapel. This is Widford's single-celled church, the last remnant of an abandoned medieval village complete with ancient and large-scale wall paintings. Traces of the lanes and houses that stood here before the Black Death devastated the village in the Middle Ages can be clearly seen in the odd lumps and bumps across the field surrounding the chapel. It stands in an idyllic location.

Most fascinating of all, a complete Roman mosaic lies beneath the church. The old church flagstones are sometimes lifted in one or two places so visitors can see traces of the mosaic, which is believed to have been part of a Roman villa. It's thought that the church builders decided to build here precisely because they wanted to show physically, as well as metaphorically, how Christianity had supplanted, and would dominate forever, the old pagan Roman ways.

Widford church is still used occasionally for services and it still has its 18th-century box pews.

St Oswald's Church is all that remains of an abandoned medieval village.

SECRETS

While you're there

Visit nearby **SWINFORD**, best known as the childhood home of the Mitford sisters.

CHEDWORTH ROMAN VILLA, just 14 miles away, continues the mosaic theme with the country's largest Roman villa.

Secret place to stay

THE FLEECE, Witney (fleecewitney.co.uk). A highly rated B&B that is locally supported.

Ickworth House

SUFFOLK

Frederick Hervey (1730–1803), Bishop of Derry and fourth Earl of Bristol, was an obsessive traveller and collector who built Ickworth House simply so he had somewhere to put his vast collection of treasures. Hervey's eccentric journeys through Europe help explain the number of Hotel Bristols all over Europe – his name became associated with a particular standard of quality. The eccentric Earl (who was noted for his fondness for leap-frogging over the backs of lesser ecclesiastics) poured much of his personality into Ickworth, though it remained unfinished at his death.

Basing his designs on Italian architecture, Hervey had Ickworth built with a central rotunda and two large curving wings, but what most concerned him was not that the house should be comfortable for people to live in, but that it should provide a suitable setting for the pictures by Velázquez, Titian and Gainsborough that he collected obsessively. The pictures and other collections – most notably of exquisite Georgian silver and fine Regency furniture – remain to this day.

The gardens would not be familiar to Hervey as they were commissioned early in the 19th century by the First Marquess of Bristol who also created the Victorian Stumpery and the Temple Rose Garden. However, the first earl's summer house and ornamental canal survive. Beyond the gardens lie the wooded park without which no 18th-century house was considered complete.

Ickworth House has a huge central dome.

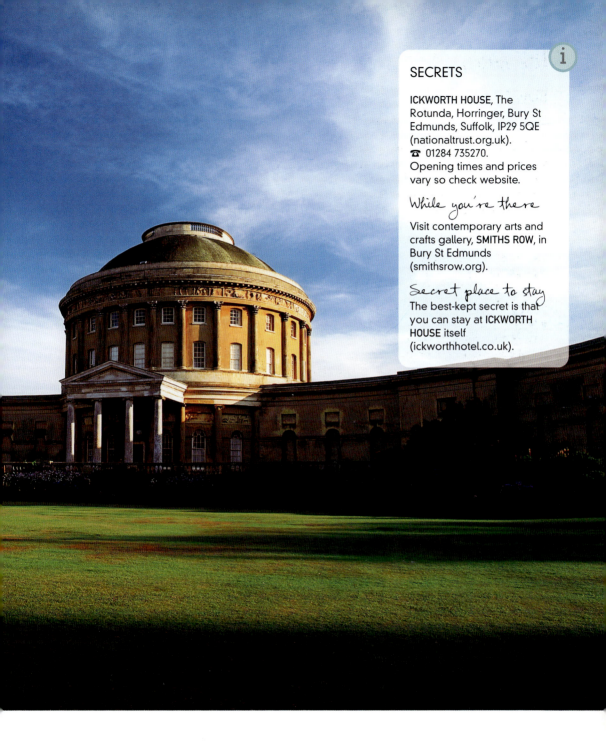

SECRETS

ICKWORTH HOUSE, The Rotunda, Horringer, Bury St Edmunds, Suffolk, IP29 5QE (nationaltrust.org.uk).
☎ 01284 735270.
Opening times and prices vary so check website.

While you're there

Visit contemporary arts and crafts gallery, **SMITHS ROW**, in Bury St Edmunds (smithsrow.org).

Secret place to stay

The best-kept secret is that you can stay at **ICKWORTH HOUSE** itself (ickworthhotel.co.uk).

The Nutshell

SUFFOLK

Whatever the claims of various pubs to be either the oldest, the biggest or the smallest in the country, there is no doubt that the Nutshell in Bury St Edmunds is a very small pub indeed. On the other hand it is not too small to provide a permanent home for its very own ghost – a little boy believed to have been murdered several centuries ago is regularly spotted toward closing time flitting up or down the stairs.

Built on three floors, the public drinking area measures just 4.5 x 2m (15 x 7ft) – that's just 30.5m^2 (100ft^2) of drinking space! The pub is not that old – though timber-framed in the style of most ancient Suffolk buildings it was probably put up early in the 19th century.

The Nutshell justifiably claims to be the smallest pub in England.

Despite its small size the pub once managed to achieve a new world record by squeezing 102 customers and one dog into the bar.

The *Guinness Book of Records* accepts the Nutshell's claim to be the smallest in the country and, in keeping with the spirit of commercialism, the pub now houses the world's smallest dartboard, as well as a stuffed three-legged chicken and a mummified cat.

SECRETS

THE NUTSHELL PUB, The Traverse, Bury St Edmunds, Suffolk, IP33 1BJ (thenutshellpub.co.uk).

While you're there

Visit **MOYSE'S HALL MUSEUM**, Cornhill. The oldest house in Bury, this Norman building is now a local history museum (stedmundsbury.gov.uk).

Secret place to stay

SWAN, Lavenham (theswanatlavenham.co.uk). Lavenham is one of Suffolk's most beautiful small medieval towns and The Swan is its most attractive ancient hotel.

Tattingstone
Wonder SUFFOLK

This is without question one of the most wonderfully eccentric buildings in the country. Originally two red-brick farmworkers' cottages, it was transformed when the local landowner, Edward White, decided he wanted a better, more religious view from his house, Tattingstone Place. So in 1790 he built a third cottage on the end of the first two, with a square flint-built church tower on top.

What makes this bizarre group of buildings so intriguing is that, looked at from one side they appear to be just an ordinary group of cottages; it's only from the other side that the fake church tower makes the whole thing look like a medieval church – which is

SECRETS

While you're there

Visit the **ANCIENT HOUSE** in nearby Ipswich. It has one of the finest examples of 15th-century pargetting – decorative plasterwork – on its front wall.

Secret place to stay

THE GREAT HOUSE RESTAURANT AND HOTEL, Lavenham, Suffolk (greathouse.co.uk/).
☎ 01284 735270.

precisely the effect the local squire intended. The Wonder can be seen from the road at the village of Tattingstone, Suffolk.

The Tattingstone Wonder looks like a church when viewed from one direction, but is actually a terrace of three cottages.

Chatley Heath Semaphore Tower

SURREY

Rapid communications systems are not entirely the preserve of the modern world – which is precisely why the Chatley Heath Semaphore Tower is so interesting. It's not the sort of place that tourists rush to, which is a great pity because, apart from the fascinating exhibitions in the tower itself (about early naval communication), there are 283ha (700 acres) of beautiful grounds that offer glorious views north to London and out across the North Downs.

The 18m (60ft) semaphore tower was built in 1822 and was one of a chain of towers

The tower gives excellent views of the grounds.

built by the Navy for communication between the Admiralty in London and the fleet at Portsmouth. As the signal on the top of each tower could instantly be seen by the signal recorder at the next tower, who then passed it on, communication would have been remarkably fast, even by today's standards.

You can stand on the platform where the tower superintendent would have stood, telescope in hand to spot the last signal, and you can even see how the semaphore mast was originally used.

SECRETS

CHATLEY HEATH SEMAPHORE TOWER
Pointers Road, Cobham, Surrey, KT11 1PQ
(visitsurrey.com/site/things-to-do/chatley-heath-semaphore-tower-p61933).
☎ 01483 795440. Open all year.
Price: adult £3, child free.

While you're there

The **NORTH DOWNS WAY**, one of Britain's less well known long-distance paths, runs nearby. Try walking it for an hour or so and you will be amazed at how rural this part of Surrey is, despite its proximity to London.

Secret place to eat

THE RUNNING HORSE, Leatherhead
☎ 01373 372081. Old-world charm, family and dog-friendly traditional English pub.

Holmbury Hill

SURREY

Holmbury Hill is part of the three-hill chain – Holmbury, Leith and Pitch – that looks over miles of wooded weald. It is a place that gives the lie to the idea that Surrey is entirely made up of stockbroker-belt housing and arterial roads, for this is remarkably wild country given how close it is to the capital.

The area is rich in woodland plants and animals, as well as heathland birds and even rare snakes. At the top of the hill you can enjoy breathtaking views and the sight of an occasional kestrel hovering overhead. The whole area is cared for by the Hurtwood Control, a unique organization whose purpose is to keep this privately owned countryside open to the public. The wooded slopes are criss-crossed by footpaths and bridleways and wherever you go there is a sense of history: the pattern of ancient settlement can still be seen – ancient hill fort remnants on the hilltops, medieval villages in the valleys, isolated farms and country houses.

SECRETS

While you're there

THE KINGS HEAD, Pitland Street, Holmbury
☎ 01306 730282. Located on the site of a very old ale house, it has been a pub since the early 19th century. Tucked in a tiny side street away from the main village road, you may come across it only by accident, or after a good walk on Holmbury Hill.

LEITH HILL with its gothic tower is a short walk away. Climb to the top for exceptional views over the surrounding counties of England.

Secret place to stay

WOTTON HOUSE VENUE, Dorking (wottonhousedorking.co.uk). Set in 8ha (20 acres) of spectacular grounds, it was once the 17th-century family home of botanist, John Evelyn.

The Surrey hills were once the inspiration for 18th- and 19th-century poets and landscape painters, who flocked to the three hills.

On top of Holmbury Hill.

Chaldon Church

SURREY

The ancient church at Chaldon in Surrey has all the look and feel of the Dark Ages, largely because of the size and condition of its magnificent 5.2m (17ft)-long medieval mural. The painting covers the whole of the west wall and, despite the long centuries during which it was hidden beneath ever-deepening layers of whitewash, it survives in superlative condition. It depicts the Day of Judgement and Ladder of Salvation, showing white figures on an ochre background, and we see how the righteous are saved and the damned sent to hell for eternity. If our medieval ancestors believed such scenes existed in reality in the afterlife, it is no wonder they flocked regularly to church.

A church was recorded on this site in the early 8th-century Charter of Frithwald, but

The great medieval painting at Chaldon.

the present building dates mostly to the mid-1100s. Originally just a simple rectangular nave, it grew in size over the centuries, but still reflects the aspirations of a humble community far from the great centres of wealth and power.

When one considers that 98 percent of all medieval religious art was destroyed during the Reformation – and almost all medieval English art was religious – the survival of this large picture is all the more miraculous. It was discovered under layers of paint during restoration work in the 1860s and entirely justifies the church's Grade I listing.

SECRETS

While you're there

Don't miss **TOLLSWORTH MANOR HOUSE** also in Chaldon. A wonderful old building with 15th and 16th century, and later, additions. Only the gardens are open to the public occasionally to raise money for charity, but the property is well worth seeing from the outside.

Secret place to stay

WHYTE HART HOTEL, Bletchingley (whytehartehotelbletchingley.co.uk). Not too far away and a good mix of the old and new.

Headley Heath

SURREY

Common land is now rare in Britain. Yet before the great period of enclosure at the end of the 18th century much of Britain was still common land. This meant it was unfenced and by ancient tradition available to villagers to graze their animals and to collect animals' (and human) bedding and firewood. The great lords who owned the estates round about passed legislation to take the commons from the ordinary villagers. Tens of thousands of acres vanished into private ownership. But one or two remnants of what was once a widespread system of land management and control do remain – one of the very best, and least visited, is Headley Heath near the much better known Box Hill.

Over 200ha (500 acres) here – the biggest remaining area of acid heathland on the North Downs – were acquired by the National Trust in 1946 from the lord of the manor, who had allowed local people to continue to exercise their ancient grazing rights. The land had never been ploughed but bracken and scrubby trees had encroached on what had been open grazing country, and it was only after a lengthy period of restoration by the Trust that Headley Heath returned to the appearance it would have had in earlier times. A key part of the Trust's restoration project was the introduction of Highland cattle.

Headley Heath's common land.

Leith Hill

SURREY

Far less well known than it should be, Leith Hill, the highest point in the south-east of England, is just 11m (35ft) lower than it needs to be to count as a mountain.

It's a lovely and spectacular spot with a colourful and hugely entertaining history. In 1765 the owner of the hill, Richard Hull, decided that it should break the magic 305m (1,000ft) barrier by hook or by crook, so he added a folly in the shape of a tower (taking the hill to 325m/1,069ft) from which he and his friends could look out across 13 counties. Visitors can still take in the views from the tower today.

Even less well known than the tower itself is the beautiful surrounding land – the ancient wooded slopes and nearby heathland known as Dukes Warren and Coldharbour Common, are both rich in wildlife, rare plants, flowers and quiet walks. In fact, this whole area – now looked after by the National Trust – is an astonishing haven of peace and quiet: the sort of place you would expect to find deep in Shropshire or Devon. The oak and hazel woods at Leith Hill are filled with bluebells in spring and rhododendrons in May and June, as well as rare woodland herbs like sweet woodruff and yellow archangel. Butterflies include the rare white admiral and there are treecreepers, nuthatches and wood warblers to be seen among other birds.

Leith Hill's folly tower.

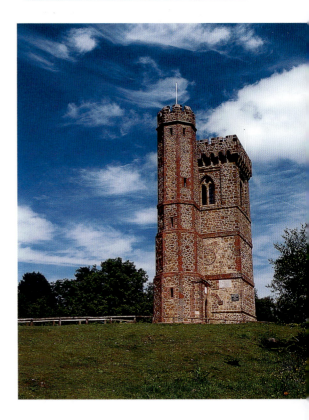

St Botolph's Church SUSSEX

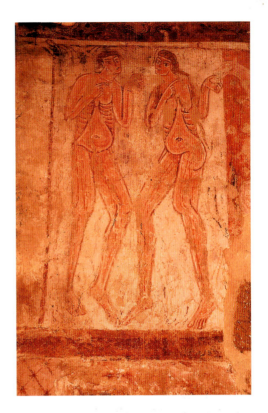

One of St Botolph's exceptional paintings.

Almost every aspect of churchgoing today would be unfamiliar to our medieval ancestors. But, if you want to see what the interior walls of every parish church in the country would have looked like before Henry VIII fell out with the Pope visit this tiny little-known church.

St Botolph's is largely Norman; it's very small because more than 900 years ago this was a remote and very poor rural community. However, the importance of the church in out-of- the-way places like this can be judged by St Botolph's wall paintings. Other churches have more spectacular individual wall paintings but none has retained virtually all its original work in the way that St Botolph's has. Virtually every surface – from the sides of the nave to the chancel arch and the altar – is covered with beautifully executed scenes from the Life of Christ, as well as extraordinary pictures of Adam and Eve, including one showing Eve milking a cow;

another picture shows the serenity of heaven and the horrors of hell. The apostles are portrayed, as well as St George slaying the dragon.

The point to remember about these curious works of art is that they were painted to instruct an illiterate population about the Bible. It is believed the St Botolph's images were the work of a group of painters working around 1100. It is ironic that the whitewash that eventually covered the pictures, and which was discovered and removed in the late 19th century, actually helped preserve them for us today. The church has also managed to retain its ancient bell.

SECRETS

While you're there

Visit the RSPB's **PULBOROUGH BROOKS NATURE RESERVE** (rspb.org.uk/reserves/ guide/p/pulboroughbrooks). Admission is free. There are walks aplenty in which to appreciate England's flora and fauna.

Secret place to stay

LYTHE HILL HOTEL, Haslemere, Surrey (lythehill.co.uk). Expensive but secluded.

Cissbury Ring

SUSSEX

It's easy to see why ancient people built their hill forts on this high chalk promontory on the South Downs, with its breathtaking views across to the Isle of Wight and to Beachy Head. When the valleys were dangerous, thickly wooded places it made sense to build forts on these high tops. And what remains of the Cissbury Iron Age hill fort is still impressive, even today thousands of years after it was first built – the ancient ditch and ramparts enclose some 26ha (65 acres), which suggests that this was a strategically important place. The inner ring alone is more than 1.6km (1 mile) long.

Beneath the hill there is evidence too of earlier peoples. Stone Age tribes, using only antler picks, dug shafts (some as deep as 12m/40ft) and tunnels here in search of flint. More than 60,000 tonnes of chalk must have been moved to build the inner bank, but sometime between BC50 and 50AD the fort was abandoned. The timber palisades and huts that were part of the fort would have crumbled and vanished leaving the earthworks we see today.

The view from the hill fort is much today as it would have been when the fort was newly built. For the modern visitor there are other pleasures – the sight, for example, of grassland plants such as cowslip and horseshoe vetch, butterflies such as the chalkhill blue and several wonderful species of orchid – particularly look out for the pyramidal.

The ancient ditch of Cissbury Ring.

SECRETS

While you're there

Nip into Worthing to see the beautiful **PARSONAGE ROW COTTAGES** in Tarring High Street. The area has superb examples of late 15th-century houses of medieval close-timbered construction.

Secret place to stay

FINDON MANOR HOTEL, Findon (findonmanor.com).
On the edge of the South Downs, this hotel is quiet, reasonably priced and has wonderful views.

Parham House

SUSSEX

This beautiful Elizabethan manor house is less well known than many similar houses because it has never been taken into public ownership. Three families have owned Parham since building began in 1577: the Palmers, the Bishops and the Pearsons.

Little changed or damaged over the years, the many-gabled stone house is filled with Elizabethan furniture and early pictures. There is a spectacular gallery more than 49m (160ft) long that would have been used to hang family portraits, and the great hall is much as it would have been when William Shakespeare was alive. A great hall was a room no Elizabethan gentleman would do without, for it was here he showed his friends and colleagues that he was a man of means.

The gardens, including the 121ha (300 acre) deer park, are equally fascinating. The herd of fallow deer roaming the park are descendants of animals introduced here in the 1620s, and the 2.8ha (7 acre) pleasure garden – an 18th-century creation – has a lake, rare trees and a wonderful brick-and-turf maze.

Among the most interesting paintings, the house contains a remarkable work by England's greatest animal painter, George Stubbs (1724–1806). Working just from the skin and skull that had been sent to him, (since no live example had ever been seen in Europe at that time,) Stubbs produced what is almost certainly the first likeness of a kangaroo in England.

Elizabethan Parham House and Gardens is still a family residence.

SECRETS

PARHAM HOUSE, Storrington, nr Pulborough, West Sussex RH20 4HS. (parhaminsussex.co.uk). ☎ 01903 742021. Open: House Apr–Sep Wed, Thurs, Fri, Sun & BH Mon 14.00–1700; Aug also Tues, Fri; Oct Sun 14.00–1700. Gardens Wed, Thurs, Fri, Sun & BH Mon 12.00–1700; May–Aug also Tues, Fri, Oct Sun. Price: House and garden: adult £9, child £4.50, family £26. Gardens only: adult £7, child £3.50, family £19.

While you're there

The old Downland village of **BRAMBER** on the river Adur contains the remains of a Norman castle, a beautiful 15th-century timber house, St Mary's, and the 11th-century church of St Nicholas.

Secret place to stay

VILLAGE HOUSE, Findon (villagehousefindon.co.uk). Warm, cosy and traditional.

Chyngton Farm

SUSSEX

Leaving the ancient Cinque port of Seaford on the Sussex coast and heading east you quickly reach the Cuckmere estuary and its ancient salt marsh and wetland. The Cuckmere estuary has no modern coastal town or urban development of any kind, which makes it unique among the rivers of the south coast. And here, close to where the river meanders into the sea, is Chyngton Farm. Chyngton gets its name from the medieval settlement that once existed here before the Black Death took its toll, and the growth of what is now the town of Seaford in the Middle Ages led to its being abandoned. Nothing now remains of the settlement.

The National Trust, aware of the rarity of this quiet, unspoilt landscape in the busiest corner of England, manages the land in such a way that controlled incursion by the sea has

View towards Seven Sisters Cliff.

regenerated the typical salt-marsh environment, which is now home to thousands of wading birds and duck – from plover to curlew, redshank, wigeon, teal and mallard. Songbirds are also abundant here – particularly yellowhammer – and high in the skies you are likely to see a number of birds of prey including sparrowhawk, peregrine falcon and kestrel.

The farm is criss-crossed by water-filled ditches that are home to countless species of insect including jewel-bright dragonflies and damselflies, while down at the edge of the sea on the shingle bank visitors will find plants like sea kale and sea lavender.

Chyngton is believed to be the last farm in England to have used oxen to pull carts and ploughs. Photographs taken in the 1930s show the ox teams still at work as they would have been 1,000 years earlier.

SECRETS

While you're there

Enjoy a walk, cycle or horse ride on the **SOUTH DOWNS WAY**, which runs westward from Eastbourne for 160km (100 miles) and more. It's a great place to spend a few days, or for the more active, the whole trail may reasonably be walked in approximately 6–9 days.

Secret place to stay

SWAN HOUSE HOTEL, Hastings (swanhousehastings.co.uk)
Right in the heart of the old town.

Bateman's

SUSSEX

Rudyard Kipling lived at Bateman's from 1902 until the end of his life in 1936, and when you first see the rich sandstone house that was built in 1634, it is easy to see why. Surrounded by the Sussex Weald, the house is set in a quiet location that allowed for the privacy of its owner. Bateman's was built for a local iron-master who was well off but by no means aristocratic, and its most immediately striking feature is the six-column central chimney stack.

Kipling tried to make the house look as it would have done when it was first built. He filled it with early furniture, including his own 17th-century writing table and, of course, with artefacts collected from the place that inspired so much of his writing: India. He made sure his book-lined study – his

Bateman's characterful outbuildings.

workroom – was situated right in the heart of the house, at the top of the main staircase. Here he wrote 'If' and, among other stories and poems, *Puck of Pook's Hill*.

Pens, pipes, and even Kipling's Rolls Royce are still here, together with the shallow pond he built. A tradition grew up that visitors, where necessary, should put 'FIP' after their names in the visitors' book – he abbreviation stood for 'fell in pond'.

Mrs Kipling left the house to the National Trust in 1939 with a stipulation that it should be kept as her husband had known it. The inscription on Kipling's sundial summed up his view of life: 'It is later than you think'.

SECRETS

BATEMAN'S, Bateman's Lane, Burwash, East Sussex, TN19 7DS ☎ 01435 882302. Open: House mid-Mar–Oct Mon, Tues, Wed, Sat, Sun 11–17.00; 3–18 Dec Sat, Sun 11.30–15.30. Price: adult £8.15, child £4.05, family £20.50.

While you're there

Don't miss **SMALLHYTHE PLACE**, home of Victorian actress Ellen Terry (nationaltrust.org.uk).

Secret place to stay

LEEFORD PLACE HOTEL, Battle (leefordplace.co.uk). Beautiful setting in historic countryside.

Jack Fuller's Pyramid SUSSEX

The village of Brightling, with its surrounding beechwoods, lies in one of the loveliest parts of Sussex, and it was here that Jack Fuller (1757–1834), the son of minor gentry, inherited Brightling Park.

Though he shunned publicity and, at one point in his life, refused a knighthood, Fuller was determined not to be forgotten. Like the ancient Egyptians before him, he thought that one sure way to ensure his immortality was to build a pyramid, so that's precisely what he did. But not content with a pyramid, Fuller also built a steeple, and two domes.

The pyramid in Brightling churchyard is the most interesting of Fuller's follies – the work was supervised by Sir Robert Smirke, the architect who designed the British Museum, and the pyramid stands 8m (25ft) high and 24m (80ft) round. Carefully constructed from large, precision-cut blocks of stone, it was completed in 1811 as Fuller's mausoleum but decades before he died. The pyramid was rumoured to contain the mummified body of the man himself sitting bolt upright in a chair, though this was later discovered to be untrue!

Fuller, who later became an MP, was considered eccentric even in his own lifetime. He built a 20m (65ft)-high stone obelisk, the Brightling Needle, on a nearby hill, though the reason why is unclear. Following a bet with a neighbour that he could see the church spire at Dallington from his home, and then realising that he couldn't, he built an 11 m (35ft)-high spire-shaped cone, called the Sugar Loaf, in the direction of Dallington to fool the neighbour and win the bet.

Jack Fuller is buried beneath the pyramid.

SECRETS

While you're there

Visit nearby **BODIAM CASTLE**. One of the most famous and glorious castles in Britain, complete with turrets and moat. Bodiam was built in 1385 (nationaltrust.org.uk). ☎ 01580 830196.

Secret place to stay

THE BRICKWALL HOTEL, Sedlescombe (brickwallhotel.com). ☎ 01424 870253. Beautifully set and with origins in the 16th century.

ENGLAND

Central

CENTRAL ENGLAND GIVES you the chance to visit some of the least well-known but most extraordinary survivals of our industrial past from Quaker-inspired Bournville on the outskirts of Birmingham to Soho House, where some of the great figures of the Industrial Revolution met. There are also early glassworks and, in Lincolnshire, the remarkable Maud Foster Windmill. In Nottinghamshire don't miss Mr Straw's House, a unique survival of a terraced house from the early 20th century. And at Laxton, again in Nottinghamshire, you can see the only surviving medieval field system in Britain.

Weaver Hall Museum & Workhouse CHESHIRE

Britain's coal-mining industry is famous all over the world, but what of salt mining? This little-known industry was and is the preserve of the county of Cheshire – the only place in the UK where salt is commercially produced.

The value of salt in earlier times can be judged by the fact that the word 'salary' derives from the Latin word for salt (*salis*), for this was once a commodity of enormous value. Salt was taxed heavily – in 1905 at £30 a ton – the equivalent would be £2870 today. It was also traded across Europe and used as a method of payment.

The vast salt deposits were laid down 200 million years ago and have been mined at least since Roman times. To mine the salt, shafts were dug to the 30m (98ft)-thick bands of salt

SECRETS

WEAVER HALL MUSEUM AND WORKHOUSE
162 London Road, Northwich, CW9 8AB
(weaverhallmuseum.org.uk/).
☎ 01606 271640. Open: Jan–Oct Tues–Fri
10.00–17.00, Sat, Sun 14.00–16.00; Nov–Dec
Tues–Fri 10.00–16.00, Sat, Sun 13.00–1600.
Price: adult £2.50, child £1.30.

While you're there

Visit ARLEY HALL with its wonderful gardens and fascinating Victorian house (arleyhallandgardens.com). ☎ 01565 777353. Open: April to Sept 11.00–17.00, Sun and BH.

Secret place to stay

HARTFORD HALL, Northwich
(hartfordhallpub.co.uk).
A delightful old house.

lying 37m (120ft) beneath the ground. The salt was dissolved by flooding the shafts, but as a result the overlying rock collapsed, providing an explantion for subsidence in the area.

Weaver Hall Museum helps keep the history of the salt-mining industry alive and the details of how, where and by whom it was once extracted from deep beneath the Cheshire landscape. The museum, housed in what was once the Northwich Union Workhouse, has an amazing collection of archive photographs, dating back to the late 1860s, showing the salt miners at work, the tools that they used and the conditions under which they worked. Tools and artefacts involved in the trade are exhibited, along with a number of models showing how the mines were operated.

The Northwich Union Workhouse.

Alderley Edge

CHESHIRE

This is a fascinating area, rich in wildlife and with remarkable geology. The Edge itself is a wooded slope from the top of which are the best views in Cheshire – you can see across the whole of the Cheshire Plain on a clear day. The area west of the ancient wooded slope is owned – like the Edge itself – by the National Trust, and here you will find old pasture mixed with stands of trees and nationally rare areas of heathland. These provide a home for numerous threatened species of moth and butterfly, which thrive on the heather and bilberry that predominates on this unspoilt landscape.

There are ancient oaks and to the west beech, ash and pine trees. Throughout the area

View east across the Cheshire Plain.

SECRETS

While you're there

Visit the nearby WIZARD INN, which commemorates a legend about Merlin guarding the entrance to one of the numerous caves.

Secret place to stay

ALDERLEY EDGE HOTEL, Alderley Edge (alderleyedgehotel.com).
A great restaurant and pretty grounds.

deer, fox, badger and numerous woodland bird species may be glimpsed by the keen-eyed.

Like much of Cheshire the underlying geology here is a fascinating maze of mineshafts and tunnels – lead and copper have been mined at Alderley since the Bronze Age and much of the deep network probably remains to be discovered. The Trust looks after the caves which are regularly explored by local caving clubs.

Riley's Graves

DERBYSHIRE

Eyam village is well known to students of social history, but hidden away in a remote part of Derbyshire it deserves to be better known by the general public, for the story of Eyam is a tale of ordinary country people who had to face one of the most dreadful diseases in human history: bubonic plague.

The village sits just below Eyam Moor in the Derwent Valley, with a Norman church and many old houses. In the high street Eyam Hall, built in 1676 is still home to the Wright family, who built it and whose ancestors would have lived and died in the plague that visited the village in the middle decades of the 17th century.

Eyam was at that time home to the Talbot and Hancock families, whose graves now lie just outside the village. The Graves are called Riley's graves from 'roylee' (the name of a plot of land). The Hancocks lived in a house near the graves though nothing now remains of their home. The written records tell us that Elizabeth Hancock cared for and buried her six children and her husband as each fell victim to the plague. It was only then that she abandoned the house. A similar fate overtook the Talbots and many others in the village.

But what makes Eyam so tragic is that once the plague was known to be among the villagers, everyone agreed voluntarily not to try to escape, but instead to stay and cut themselves off from the rest of the world. For this was 1665, the year in which London was devastated by a similar outbreak.

The church at Eyam.

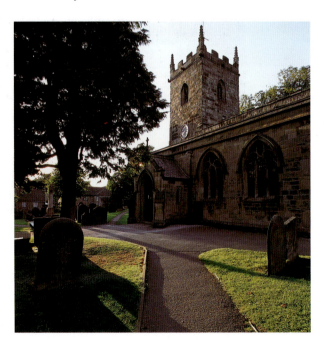

SECRETS

While you're there

Visit the **MINER'S ARMS** in Eyam. It was built in 1630 and is said to be the most haunted building in England.

EYAM HALL is open for visitors for just two months of the year. Check the website for guided tour dates, times and prices (eyamhall.co.uk).

Secret place to stay

GEORGE HOTEL, Youlgreave ☎ 01629 636292. Traditional pub serving great food.

Buxton Opera House DERBYSHIRE

When people think of opera they think of the great metropolitan centres – London, Milan, Sydney – but hidden away in the north of England, specifically that glorious part of Derbyshire on the edge of the Peak District, is an opera house that can stand comparison with the best in the world.

A classic piece of Edwardian architecture, Buxton Opera House was lucky to survive the long period during the 1960s and 1970s when Britain became obsessed by television, but survive it did (despite being used as a cinema for some years), and it has recently been restored to its original Edwardian splendour.

It was built by Frank Matcham in 1903. Matcham specialized in building music halls and theatres – his most famous buildings, apart from the Buxton Opera House are the London Coliseum and the Hackney Empire, the latter being one of the last remaining of the old music halls.

Despite being tucked away in this corner of Derbyshire, Buxton Opera House has attracted some of the greatest names in entertainment history – Anna Pavlova performed here in 1935 and Gracie Fields and Hermione Gingold were regulars. The Buxton Opera Festival, based around the opera house, is now held every year and visitors are invariably astonished at the beauty of their surroundings – the opera house is set in 10ha (25 acres) of ornamental gardens and the old spa town of Buxton is all around you.

The imposing façade of Buxton Opera House.

SECRETS

BUXTON OPERA HOUSE, Water Street, Buxton, Derbyshire, SK17 6XN (buxtonoperahouse.org.uk).

While you're there

Don't miss the chance to get up on the hills as you are very close here to the **PEAK DISTRICT NATIONAL PARK.** (peakdistrict.gov.uk/visiting) ☎ 01629 816200.

Secret place to stay

OLD HALL HOTEL, Buxton (oldhallhotelbuxton.co.uk). It claims to be the oldest hotel in the country. Certainly it is ancient (Mary, Queen of Scots reputedly stayed here). The hotel offers a good base from which to see the town and surrounding countryside.

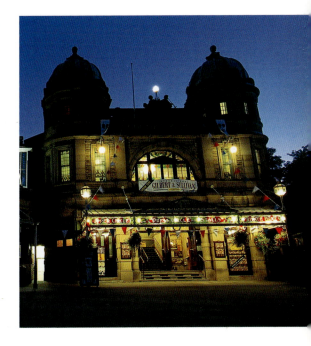

Speedwell Cavern

DERBYSHIRE

A narrow entrance takes you down more than 100 steps from Winnats Pass – high up in the remote Peak District – to an incredible underground world that nothing above ground could ever have prepared you for.

SECRETS

SPEEDWELL CAVERN, Winnats Pass, Castleton, Hope Valley, Derbyshire S33 8WA (speedwellcavern.co.uk). Open: April–Oct 10.00–17.00; Nov-Mar 10.00–14.00. Price: adult £9.25, child £7.25, family £31.00.

While you're there

Visit the ruins of **PEVERIL CASTLE**, Castleton, finished in 1176, with its magnificent views across the Peak District (english-heritage.org.uk).

Secret place to stay

CAVENDISH HOTEL, Chatsworth Estate (cavendish-hotel.net). Stay on the estate of one of the greatest and most historic houses in England. ☎ 01246 582 311

At the bottom of the steps, is a mysterious subterranean canal dug by hand more than 200 years ago by lead miners. From here you can take a boat through this dripping, echoing underground world. The canal runs eerily through seemingly endless tunnels – the abandoned mine workings – before suddenly entering a vast system of natural caverns, lakes and rivers.

You are now hundreds of feet beneath the hills in what is just part of a huge underground system, but the best is yet to come. At last the boat reaches the incredible Bottomless Pit, a huge underground lake that lies beneath a magnificent cavern roof. Even St Paul's Cathedral pales into insignificance compared to this awe-inspiring natural cathedral.

The eerie Bottomless Pit in Speedwell Cavern.

Mam Tor

DERBYSHIRE

Few natural phenomena can compare with Mam Tor, which is in essence an extremely precarious peak standing 500m (1700 ft) high – it is so unstable, in fact, that it caused the permanent closure of the nearby A625 road in the late 1970s. Despite the best efforts of modern engineering the peak simply refuses to stay in one place! And the reason? Mam Tor is made up entirely of extremely unstable horizontal layers of shale and gritstone. These materials are particularly prone to water damage: heavy annual rainfall makes its way between the layers, freezes in winter and then expands, causing movement and providing the catalyst for landslip. The shale and gritstone continually crumbles and the mountain – in the right conditions – seems to shiver as it moves and decays.

Despite all this crumbling, you can still climb safely to the top of the Tor, where there is evidence of an Iron Age hill fort. The climb is well worth it for the views along the Hope Valley and for the sense that you have climbed a peak that is constantly on the move!

Mam Tor is known as the Shivering Mountain.

Calke Abbey

DERBYSHIRE

Most National Trust houses have a well-kept, beautifully manicured appearance that demonstrate the landmarks at their finest hour, but in recent years there has been a move toward displaying houses − whether stately homes or smaller buildings − as they might have been at the time that they were last lived in − in this case, in a state of decline and neglect known as 'arrested decay'.

Originally the site of a monastery (hence its name), Calke Abbey − the second largest house in Derbyshire − started its domestic life as a Tudor house, but was rebuilt in the 18th century. What makes it unique is the extraordinary family that owned it over the centuries. For more than 300 years generation after generation inherited the house until crippling death duties forced the family to relinquish it to the National Trust.

The Harpurs made their fortune as lawyers in the late 16th century, and were notoriously reclusive, discouraging visitors to the house. Over the years they collected a vast amount of paraphernalia including furniture, books, pictures, toys, wall hangings, and even carriages, as well as a natural history collection of stuffed birds and eggs. As objects accumulated nothing was ever thrown away: until eventually the clutter filled the main rooms, storerooms, cupboards, corridors and even the attic.

Calke Abbey is preserved as it was found. Though shabby in places, it offers a rare glimpse of an eccentric family home.

SECRETS

CALKE ABBEY, Ticknall, Derby, Derbyshire DE73 7LE (nationaltrust.org.uk). ☎ 01332 863822. Open: House Feb–Oct Mon, Tues, Wed, Sat, Sun 12.30–17.00. Garden end Feb–mid-Apr Mon, Tues, Wed, Sat, Sun 11.00–17.00; mid-Apr–Oct 11.00–17.00. Price: House and garden: adult £10, child £5, family £25.27. Garden only: adult £6.18, child £3.09, family £15.90.

While you're there

Visit the remarkable National Trust **MUSEUM OF CHILDHOOD** at Sudbury Hall, Sudbury.

Secret place to stay

THE ROYAL HOTEL, Ashby de la Zouche (royalhotelashby.com). Built at the beginning of the 19th century, it is a comfortable and historically interesting hotel.

Croft Ambrey and Croft Castle

HEREFORDSHIRE

A hill community lived at Croft Ambrey for more than 1,000 years, from about BC1100 to roughly 50AD. What began life as a triangular Iron Age hill fort was extended over the centuries – most notably in about BC390 when archaeological evidence suggests the site increased from about 1ha (2½ acres) to more than 2ha (5 acres). At this time rows of huts were built and massive ramparts added. Animals were kept on the site and there is evidence of weaving and grain storage. To the north a steep slope would have given the original inhabitants wide views over the surrounding landscape and provided early warning of attack. In total, the site was rebuilt, expanded or modified up to 15 times.

Below the Hill Fort, Croft Castle – actually a fortified house – looks out over stunning countryside and the river Lugg. The castle was heavily remodelled in the 18th century but its outer appearance suggests 14th and 15th century work. It is specially noted for its ornate plaster ceilings. There is a lovely walled garden and an avenue of sweet chestnuts. The castle remained in the Croft family – they'd lived here since before the Norman Conquest – until 1746, when it was sold to repay huge debts. Amazingly a Croft – a descendant of the original family – bought the house in 1923, and although now looked after by the National Trust, it is still lived in by members of the family.

Croft Ambrey has been built and rebuilt.

SECRETS

CROFT CASTLE AND PARKLAND, Yarpole, near Leominster, Herefordshire, HR6 9PW (nationaltrust.org.uk). ☎ 01568 782120. Opening times and ticket prices vary, so check the website.

While you're there

The nearby **MEDIEVAL CHURCH** of St Michael and All Angels has a magnificent Croft tomb dating from the early 16th century.

Secret place to stay

OVERTON GRANGE HOTEL, Ludlow (overtongrangehotel.com). A splendid little place to stay just 8km (5 miles) from Croft.

Loughborough Bell Foundry

LEICESTERSHIRE

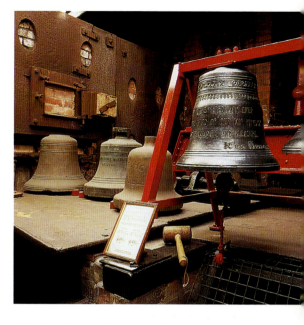

Bells have been made in the same way for centuries, and the technology has changed little. In Britain's thousands of churches bells still need to be regularly repaired or replaced. As a result, bellfounders tend to survive where other ancient manufactures have long since vanished. Though it has passed through a number of families, the bell foundry at Loughborough, owned by the Taylor family since 1784, has been in business continuously since the 14th century. For hundreds of years

Bells have been made in Loughborough since medieval times.

bells have been sent from Taylors all over the world. The biggest bell ever cast – the near 16-tonne Great Paul for St Paul's Cathedral in London – was made here in 1881.

Taylors combine bell making with a bell museum devoted to the history and mystery of bells and bell making. Each bell is cast by hand by skilled workmen and every one is unique, since the mould from which each is made is broken up as part of the process. Horse manure, sand and hay are still used to make the profile for the inner core of the bell. Once the two halves of the bell are assembled, tuners working with precision remove thin pieces of metal from the bell until the correct pitch is obtained. All this and more is explained in the museum which is also devoted to hand bells, carillons and ships' bells.

The Jew's House

LINCOLNSHIRE

Grand houses, chapels and churches survive in their hundreds from the late Middle Ages and occasionally from even earlier periods, but a small town house from just after the Norman Conquest sounds too unlikely to be true. But one such house does indeed survive – and in a most unlikely setting.

Halfway down one of the narrow lanes that descend from Lincoln's great cathedral is a modest-looking stone house, now part of a much-later row of houses. Only the arcading on the front stonework of the house gives a clue to the extraordinary age of this building, for it is believed to date to just before 1100 – a date which makes it by far the oldest domestic building still in use in the country. An original chimney stack is visible above the centre of the doorway.

But how did the house get its name? It is not a pleasant story, but it is typical of Christian history. A child from the town, who later became known as Little Saint Hugh, is said to have been murdered in the Jew's House. The accusation, for which no real evidence was ever produced, led to the arrest of 90 Jewish people in the town, one of whom was coerced by torture to admit the murder. Another 18 were hanged for refusing to put themselves before a Chritian trial. The accusations were most likely prefabricated in order to fine rich Jews and raise money for the king's purse.

The Jew's House in Lincoln.

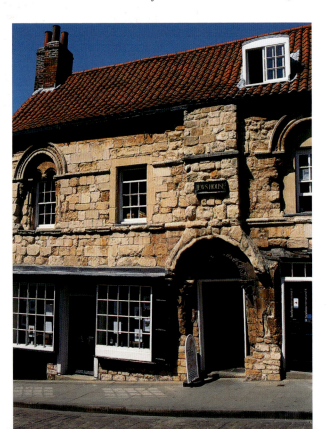

SECRETS

While you're there

Don't miss the **PARROT ZOO** at Friskney near Boston, which houses Britain's biggest collection of these wonderful birds (parrotzoo.com).

LINCOLN CATHEDRAL offers roof top tours with splendid views over the city and beyond. Climb the tower if you have th energy.

Secret place to stay

ADMIRAL RODNEY HOTEL, Horncastle (admiralrodney.com). Relatively inexpensive and rather a nice building.

Tattershall Castle

LINCOLNSHIRE

The border castles of the Welsh Marches and remote Northumberland and Scotland are well known, but even in the unlikely setting of the rich, flat lands of Lincolnshire the castle builders were occasionally at work. By the time Tattershall was built in about 1430, however, castle building had more to do with grand gestures than the threat of attack. In fact, Tattershall is actually just a grand tower house posing as a castle – it was built to reflect the wealth and power of its first owner, Ralph Cromwell (1394–1456).

Tattershall Castle is really a tower house.

It is said that more than a million bricks were used to construct the six-storey great tower, which rises to more than 33m (110ft) and gazes out across the Lincolnshire landscape. Ralph Cromwell was Lord Treasurer, which may explain how he amassed the wealth needed to build the tower at a time when bricks were extremely expensive. He probably felt he'd earned his power and position, for he fought with Henry VI in 1415 at one of history's greatest battles – Agincourt.

Maud Foster
Windmill LINCOLNSHIRE

Despite the destruction caused by the Industrial Revolution as well as modern methods of grinding corn, a surprisingly large number of ancient mills still exist. But even among those that have been restored, the Maud Foster Mill is a rare gem – it was built in 1819 and unusually, has five sails instead of four. Why this should be, no one knows. The mill is the tallest in Britain and the last in an area once noted for its windmills – an 18th-century traveller recalled the skyline in the Boston area as alive with the motions and creakings of these great creatures.

But Maud Foster – the mill gets its name from one of its first owners – is not a museum, or at least not entirely a museum. In these days when we worry far more about the quality of our food (and not just the price), Maud Foster Windmill still produces organic flour and porridge oats for sale, with regular customers across Lincolnshire and beyond.

It's a long climb to the top of the windmill, but worth it for the views (a fee is payable to climb the tower) and, as you descend, for the chance to see just how all our flour would once have been ground – the intricate mechanism of cogs and pulleys, chutes and grindstones is a tribute to the craftsmen who once travelled the country constructing and repairing these vital pieces of equipment.

Climb all seven floors of one of the tallest windmills in Britain.

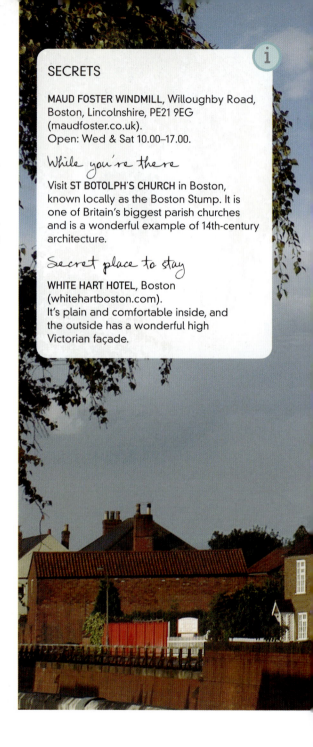

SECRETS

MAUD FOSTER WINDMILL, Willoughby Road, Boston, Lincolnshire, PE21 9EG (maudfoster.co.uk).
Open: Wed & Sat 10.00–17.00.

While you're there

Visit ST BOTOLPH'S CHURCH in Boston, known locally as the Boston Stump. It is one of Britain's biggest parish churches and is a wonderful example of 14th-century architecture.

Secret place to stay

WHITE HART HOTEL, Boston (whitehartboston.com).
It's plain and comfortable inside, and the outside has a wonderful high Victorian façade.

Gainsborough Old Hall LINCOLNSHIRE

Tucked away in the most unassuming manner in this quiet town, Gainsborough Old Hall seems to have had luck on its side. The modernizers of the 18th century left it alone, and the town planners and ring-road builders of the 1960s managed, by some miracle, to miss the chance to demolish this crooked, eminently picturesque manor house, which dates back to the 1460s.

If the survival of the building itself is a surprise, the endurance of so much of the interior is not far short of miraculous. The great hall was never modernized by the insertion of a first floor, and it is easy to imagine the local squire's men at long banqueting tables, the smoke from the central fire gradually disappearing up through the massive oak timbers of the roof. Look up today and the huge trusses and beams are still there, made from local oak cut down and shaped more than five centuries ago.

Gainsborough Old Hall is one of the most complete timber hall houses in the country.

Narrow passages lead from the great hall to a medieval kitchen, which really does still look like it belongs in that era. There are two original massive fireplaces.

SECRETS

GAINSBOROUGH OLD HALL, Parnell Street, Gainsborough, Lincolnshire, DN21 2NB (gainsboroughholdhall.co.uk).
Open: Mar–Oct; Mon–Fri 10.00–17.00, Sat 11.00–17.00, Sun 11.00–17.00.

While you're there

Go south 11km (7 miles) to the ruins of **TORKSEY CASTLE**, destroyed in the Civil War but hugely atmospheric.

Secret place to stay

WHITE HART HOTEL, Lincoln (whitehart-lincoln.co.uk).
Close to the cathedral.

Eleanor Cross

NORTHAMPTONSHIRE

When Edward I's Queen Eleanor of Castile died in 1290, her coffin was carried to London's Westminster Abbey from Harby in Nottinghamshire. In each of the places where the cortege stopped to rest at night on the long journey south, Edward later erected a cross to commemorate his dead queen. Only three of the original dozen crosses erected in 1294 survive. The best is this one at Geddington.

It stands in the middle of the village, and to most visitors it looks like a long forgotten monument of no special merit, but even after the passage of more than 700 years, a closer inspection reveals the remarkable quality of the carving on the cross; there are three niches and in each is a statue of Eleanor. Above and below her there are elaborate decorative carvings typical of English Gothic. Books with inscriptions feature in the bottom tier.

Eleanor Cross in Geddington.

SECRETS

While you're there

Visit **RUTLAND WATER** at Oakham, with its spectacular walks and bizarre half-drowned Normanton Church.

Secret place to stay

THE HIND, Wellingborough (thehind.co.uk).
You will be staying where Oliver Cromwell is once reputed to have stayed.

Church of the Holy Sepulchre

NORTHAMPTONSHIRE

Almost all the best architecture that survives from the Middle Ages, or earlier, is ecclesiastical. Among the rarest and most interesting examples of such buildings are round medieval churches. Only four of these remain in England. The least altered (though much added to) is the Church of the Holy Sepulchre in Northampton.

The church was built by the Earl of Northampton, Simon de Senlis, in about 1100, after he returned safely from the first crusade to the holy land. That he survived what must have been an incredibly long and dangerous journey is exceptional enough, but far more remarkable is his recreation in Northamptonshire of the Church of the Holy Sepulchre from Jerusalem, though at half the size of the original. This church is, in fact, a very close replica, and on entering the church you might easily be fooled into thinking you had suddenly been transported to the Middle East. It is thought that such round churches were fashionable and built as long ago as the 4th century. A similar church exists in Cambridge and it is worth comparing the two, although that church was built 30 years later.

Just inside the entrance de Senlis created a sunken circular space supported by 8 pillars – this was originally the nave – but a long chancel was added in the 13th century and the spire and tower at the end of the 14th century. George Gilbert Scott, the Victorian architect, added the apse centuries later.

De Senlis, with his wife Maud, founded a local priory and are thought to have built Northampton Castle.

The interior of Holy Sepulchre, Northampton.

SECRETS

While you're there

You're not far from the strangely named but rather lovely village of **WANSFORD-IN-ENGLAND**, where you can wander the broad main street, with its old cottages.

Secret place to stay

HAYCOCK HOTEL, Wansford-in-England (macdonaldhotels.co.uk). An old coaching inn, now converted into a hotel but retaining plenty of fascinating historical detail.

Clumber Park

NOTTINGHAMSHIRE

At one time Clumber Park was best known as the place that gave the Clumber spaniel its name. This rather sorrowful-looking animal is now very rare, but to own one was once the height of sophistication. Today the estate that gave the breed its name is still one of the glories of Nottinghamshire.

Clumber Park runs to nearly 1,620ha (4,000 acres), and it is a wonder that such a huge landholding survived the rigours of inheritance tax and falling land values. Everything about Clumber is on the biggest scale – the lime drive is 3km (2 miles) long and there is a 35ha (87-acre) lake, for example. The house, however, is long gone, demolished in the 1930s, when it proved too expensive to maintain, following the financial devastation wrought by World War I. Its spirit lives on, however, though in a thousand different locations – the fireplaces were sold off, the old panelling probably went to America, the furniture and pictures to Sotheby's, and the stone, brick and joists to a builder's yard to be recycled in other smaller houses.

The stable block did survive however, and the estate remains a gem of a place to enjoy the great outdoors with its miles of unspoilt walks, cycle rides, bridle paths, lake and trees.

The lake at Clumber Park.

SECRETS

CLUMBER PARK, North Nottinghamshire, south of Worksop, in the northernmost part of Sherwood Forest (nationaltrust.org.uk). Open: dawn til dusk. A fee is payable.

While you're there

Visit one of the National Trust's more unusual properties – the **WORKHOUSE AT SOUTHWELL**. The house provides a fascinating insight into how the poor were once treated.

Secret place to stay

SARACEN'S HEAD, Southwell (saracensheadhotel.net). An ancient and charming hotel that has recently undergone extensive refurbishment.

Mr Straw's House

NOTTINGHAMSHIRE

Of all the extraordinary houses owned by the National Trust, Mr Straw's House at 7 Blythe Grove is certainly remarkable. In outward appearance it is an ordinary semi-detached house, but inside, in every respect it is a time capsule, unchanged since the early part of the 20th century.

The story of Mr Straw's House begins when a young couple moved into the house in 1923. This successful grocer had the house decorated immediately in the most popular style of the day. But as Worksop was many miles distant from fashionable centres such as London, the style is actually more like that which was popular at the end of the 19th century. No expense was spared, from the

Even letters are a century old in this house.

latest linoleum, to Turkish rugs, knick-knacks, costly wallpapers and curtains. As the years passed the Straws changed absolutely nothing, never incorporating modern conveniences into their lives. When they died their two sons, neither of whom married, continued to live in the house and they too, chose not to make changes. When the last brother died in the early 1990s he left the house and its contents to the National Trust.

Today Mr Straw's House is exactly as it was in the early 1920s – runners, stair carpets and outside loo. Even the food cupboards contain items in tins from the 1930s. The chests of drawers are filled with beautifully preserved late Victorian linen. The brothers kept their parents' best clothes neatly folded away in cupboards and drawers, and the hats and coats on the hooks in the hall have been there since 1930!

SECRETS

MR STRAW'S HOUSE, 5–7 Blyth Grove, Worksop, Nottinghamshire, S81 0JG (nationaltrust.org.uk) ☎ 01909 482380.
Open: mid-Mar–Oct Tues–Sat 11.00–17.00.
Price: adult £6.25, child £3.10, family £15.50.

While you're there

Visit the National Trust's **STAINSBY MILL**, a working watermill that shows exactly how flour was made two centuries ago.

Secret place to stay

YE OLDE BELL, Barnby Moor (yeoldebell-hotel.co.uk).
A lovely building filled with antiques and period charm.

Laxton

NOTTINGHAMSHIRE

'Why go to see a few fields?' you might ask. 'Where's the interest in that?' The answer is that these are no ordinary fields: they are in fact the last remaining medieval agricultural system of land management in Britain.

Three big fields adjoin the village and they are still, even today, ploughed in strips, which was the system once used throughout the length and breadth of England until enclosure changed the rest of the country forever. Quite why Laxton alone kept to the old system is a mystery, but the three fields and the system by which they are farmed – first mentioned in a document of 1200 – still

Laxton fields are still farmed according to principles in place before the Enclosure Act.

have their ridge and furrow of ancient times. If you want to see what the medieval farmed countryside looked like, this is the only place you can still do it.

The Laxton Manorial Court still meets to decide on disputes over the strips of land and visitors today can choose one or more of three walks that cross these rare and special fields.

SECRETS

While you're there

Don't miss the lovely **LAXTON VILLAGE CHURCH**; it's a gem.

Secret place to stay

MARKHAM HOTEL, Markham Moor, nr Retford (markhamhotel.co.uk). This nearby hostelry has been looking after travellers for more than four centuries.

Upton Hall Time Museum

NOTTINGHAMSHIRE

What is it about clocks that so fascinates? Perhaps it is the fact that with, say, a grandfather clock it is possible to own a beautiful piece of furniture that is also a piece of ancient technology, and one that will, moreover, still adequately perform the task for which is was first designed. Whatever the reason, clock enthusiasts will not want to miss Upton Hall, a beautiful Georgian house that provides a home for the British Horological Institute and its extraordinary collection of clocks, watches and timepieces.

Here you will find exquisite 17th-century longcase clocks, clocks with automata, lantern and carriage clocks, night clocks, musical clocks of staggering complexity, moon-phase clocks, celestial clocks, clocks by world-famous makers like Knibb and Tompion, and even a Chinese incense clock. Upton Hall is also home to the atomic BBC pips machine, as well as a number of clocks that are more than three centuries old.

One of the museum's splendid clocks.

SECRETS

UPTON HALL TIME MUSEUM
Upton Hall, Upton, Newark,
Nottinghamshire, NG23 5TE
(bhi.co.uk/museum.html).
Open Sundays that mark the beginning
and end of British Summer Time and the
second weekend in June.

While you're there

Visit nearby Newark, home to one of
Britain's oldest pubs, the **PRINCE RUPERT**.
The pub has been carefully restored, even
to the extent of the walls being given a
coat of traditional lime plaster
(theprincerupert.co.uk).

Secret place to stay

GRANGE HOTEL, Newark
(grangenewark.co.uk). Small and cosy, with
an award-winning restaurant.

Clipsham Yews

RUTLAND

Apart from the fact that it is pre-eminently the tree of graveyards, the yew is also our longest-living tree, which may explain the myths and mythology that surround it. But the yew is also a popular decorative tree – largely because it is a beautiful evergreen and it can be clipped into all sorts of shapes. It was also once the timber of choice for the English longbow that most famously defeated the French at Agincourt in 1415.

Many grand houses in earlier centuries planted yew walks and avenues and one of the most impressive – and bizarre – is at Clipsham Hall. More than 150 ancient yews line the drive to the house. In the Victorian period, for reasons no one has yet quite explained, the head gardener at Clipsham, Amos Alexander, was asked to start trimming the trees into a virtual menagerie – here you will find elephants and horses, as well as abstract shapes, battle scenes and even a moon landing. The tradition that began in the 1870s continues to this day as new designs are continually added to the strange and slightly surreal collection.

The strange shapes of the Clipsham Yews.

Long Mynd

SHROPSHIRE

For fully 16km (10 miles) the high ridge of the Mynd cuts across Shropshire. Designated both as an Area of Outstanding Natural Beauty and as a Site of Special Scientific Interest, nearly 2,430ha (6,000 acres) of Long Mynd are looked after by the National Trust. The Mynd, which deserves to be as well known as many of the Lake District's upland regions, is one of the loveliest places in England to spend the day, if for no other reason than the fabulous views from the top of the Ridge to Cheshire and the Black Mountains.

Hill forts were built here in ancient times and there is evidence of human habitation from all periods – from the Bronze and Iron ages right through to the Middle Ages. This land, that was once regarded as useless and unproductive – the soils on the Mynd are thin and acidic – are now seen as rare and highly valued habitats for a range of species. Here you will find bog pimpernel and spotted orchid,

The Long Mynd is great walking country.

butterwort and bilberry among a range of rare and not-so-rare plants. Among the birds there are stonechat and ouzel, buzzard and even a few red grouse. The ridge is cut through here and there by valleys, where tracks and pathways will take you into woodlands where flycatchers and wagtails, deer and fox are left largely undisturbed.

Wenlock Edge

SHROPSHIRE

Shropshire is one of just two English counties listed by the Council for the Protection of Rural England (CPRE) as having real countryside. By 'real' they mean areas that are at least a mile or so from the nearest habitation or road. When you visit Wenlock Edge it is easy to see what the CPRE means. This thin, 24km (15 mile) escarpment runs from Ironbridge, which gets its name from the world's oldest iron bridge, to Craven Arms. The limestone ridge is a mass of fossils, for it is made of the bodies of millions of long-dead sea creatures and was once a coral reef lapped by ancient ocean waves. Tectonic plate movements over millions of years pushed up the sea bed to create the ridge we see today.

Like the Long Mynd, Wenlock is associated with that great poet of the Shropshire countryside A. E. Housman (1859–1936). In addition to the beauty of landscape celebrated by Housman, there is a vast treasure of industrial archaeology along this important Site of Special Scientific

SECRETS

While you're there

Visit **MUCH WENLOCK**, which is decidely pretty and unspoilt.

Secret place to stay

WENLOCK EDGE INN, near Much Wenlock (wenlockedgeinn.co.uk). For great food and a comfortable night.

Interest. Lime was quarried throughout the area from earliest times and limekilns – used to burn the limestone in order to make a useful fertilizer – sprang up from the Middle Ages onwards. The ancient woods were coppiced for centuries to provide fuel for the limekilns. Traces of the old workings can be seen everywhere, but the area is most valued now for its rare plants and animals: trees include wych elm, maple, ash and hazel, and among a host of rare limestone-loving plants are the wonderfully named splurge laurel, the nettle-leaved bellflower and yellow archangel.

View over Shropshire's wonderful countryside.

Cheddleton
Flint Mill STAFFORDSHIRE

See how flint was ground into powder.

The vast industrial output of the potteries during the 19th century was fuelled, in part, by long-forgotten chemical processes. Few traces of these processes remain today, but at least one has its memorial: the Cheddleton Flint Mill. The only one of its kind remaining, Cheddleton reveals a fascinating trade without which Staffordshire's world-famous potteries could not have existed.

Cheddleton is a watermill that ground flint into powder using water from the river Churnet to provide the power. The raw flint was brought to Cheddleton by boat from Kent. Once there it was loaded into kilns and burned for several days to assist the grinding process. The finely ground powder was then sent by boat along the nearby Cauldon Canal to great pottery makers such as Wedgwood and Spode, where it was mixed with clay to add vital strength to the millions of jugs, cups, mugs, plates and ornamental ware produced and sent all over the world.

Today the mill complex consists of two watermills, a drying kiln, two burning kilns and the miller's cottage. The earliest parts of the south mill date back to the 13th century, when corn was probably ground here. Most of what we see today dates back to the 18th century and the beginning of the Industrial Revolution.

SECRETS

CHEDDLETON FLINT MILL, on the A520 at Cheddleton between Stoke-on-Trent and Leek (people.exeter.ac.uk/akoutram/cheddleton-mill/). ☎ 0161 408 5083 for opening times.

While you're there

Visit nearby **CHEDDLETON STATION**, designed by the great Victorian architect Augustus Pugin, with its preserved steam railway (churnet-valley-railway.co.uk/cheddleton.htm).

Secret place to stay

RUDYARD HOTEL, nr Leek (rudyardhotel.com). Situated at the edge of Rudyard Lake, the hotel has been run by the same family for many years and is something of a landmark.

Gladstone Pottery Museum STAFFORDSHIRE

It's a small miracle that at least one part of the old potteries survives in almost pristine condition. The Gladstone Pottery Museum used to be a pottery factory and it has been kept just as it was during the early days of an industry that put Staffordshire on the world map. Gladstone is truly the last of its kind and it gives the visitor the chance to see how pottery was made in the early part of the 19th century. Arranged around a crooked cobbled yard are the curious coal-fired, bottle-shaped, brick-built kilns – works of art in themselves – that once lay at the heart of all pottery manufacture.

At Gladstone you can see the whole process from raw clay to final pot. Conditions would have been harsh for workers amid the fierce heat and dust of the process. Archive film of the last of the potters – men and women still at work in the 1930s and 1940s – is regularly shown. Visitors are encouraged to try throwing a pot themselves.

In addition to the usual run of jugs and plates, decorative tiles were made here, as well as everything from artificial flowers to lavatories. The delicate hand-painting that gave early pottery its distinctive look is carried on still by the few craftsmen who remain to show us what it was once like.

So if you want to discover exactly what a jollier, a jigger and a sagger maker once did, Gladstone is one of the few places in the world where you can still find out.

The kilns of Gladstone Pottery Museum.

SECRETS

GLADSTONE POTTERY MUSEUM, Uttoxeter Road, Longton, Stoke-on-Trent, ST3 1PQ (stokemuseums.org.uk/gpm).
☎ 01782 237777. Open: 10.00–17.00. Price: adult £6.95, child £4.75, family £20.

While you're there

Visit **ST PETER AD VINCULA** (St Peter in chains) at Stoke-on-Trent. The churchyard is the interesting feature here, where you can see the graves of some of the world's most famous potters, including Josiah Wedgwood and Josiah Spode.

Secret place to stay

THE MANOR, Cheadle (themanorcheadle.co.uk). This used to be a rectory but it is now a comfortable and reasonably priced hotel and restaurant, which retains a strong sense of the past.

Cannock Chase

STAFFORDSHIRE

The New Forest, Salisbury Plain, Dartmoor and Exmoor are all well known right across the world, but Staffordshire's greatest area of open space – Cannock Chase, an officially designated Area of Outstanding Natural Beauty – is often overlooked by those travelling north to the better-known Lake District or the Scottish hills.

Surrounded by old mining towns, like Brereton, Norton Canes and Hednesford, Cannock Chase – basically a high plateau bordered to the north by the Trent Valley and by the industrial West Midlands to the south – has a unique mix of industrial heritage and rich natural history. The origins of the Chase as a medieval hunting forest can still be glimpsed here and there where ancient trees have survived, and where areas of ancient heathland escaped the plough as well as the improvers and builders.

Henry VIII's minister William Paget was given Cannock Chase early in the 16th century. He would have overseen small-scale mining for the rich seams of coal that characterize the underlying geology, but it wasn't until the middle decades of the 19th century that mining grew exponentially. Canals and railways made the boom possible until, by the early part of the 20th century, 23,000 men carried four million tons of coal a year to the surface. But amid the dust and the dirt, the Chase survived relatively unscathed and now provides – as it did for those miners – a haven of relief from the pressures of everyday life.

Typical woodland at Cannock Chase.

SECRETS

While you're there

Visit the ruins of nearby **RUGELEY OLD CHURCH.** Dedicated to St Augustine, it has a fascinating Celtic cross in the graveyard.

Secret place to stay

LONGDEN OLD HALL FARM, nr Rugeley (longdonoldhallfarm.co.uk). A B&B in a 16th-century building set in an Area of Outstanding Natural Beauty.

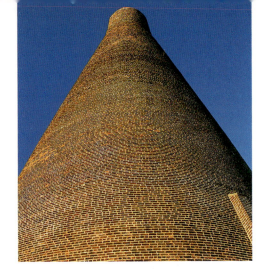

Red House Glass Cone WARWICKSHIRE

For more than four centuries glass has been made in this well-known corner of Warwickshire. The Red House Glass Cone was built in 1790 and continued in use – amazingly – until as late as 1936. The cone soars to 30m (100ft) and is basically a furnace around which the glass makers and blowers once carried on their trade. Four glass cones exist in the UK but this is the best of them in the sense that what we see now is almost exactly what was first built.

A spiral staircase takes visitors up through the cone to a viewing platform, where the curious structure can be fully appreciated. Tunnels and passageways have only recently been opened to the public and, best of all, the cone is still home to glass makers who can demonstrate the skills that kept the business going for 200 years.

ABOVE: The soaring brickwork of the glass cone.

SECRETS

RED HOUSE GLASS CONE. High Street, Wordsley, Stourbridge, DY8 4AZ (dudley.gov.uk/leisure-and-culture/museums--galleries/). Open: 10.00–16.00. Free entry.

While you're there

Visit the splendid and little-known **WOLVERHAMPTON ART GALLERY**, with its collection of pop art pictures and works by local artists (wolverhamptonart.org.uk).

Secret place to stay

TALBOT HOTEL, Stourbridge (thetalbot-hotel.co.uk). This 3-star hotel's attractive structure dates back to the 1630s.

Packwood House

WARWICKSHIRE

This 16th-century house is a fascinating example of the genuine and the fake – the basic house, by which is meant walls, floors and ceilings, is certainly Tudor. The interior however, was restored to look like a Tudor interior in the early 20th century at a time when a resurgence of interest in the architecture of that period saw 'Tudorbethan' housing estates spring up in suburbs all over the country. At Packwood House the mock Tudor is contained in the genuine article, and reveals how the architect of the 1930s perceived a Tudor house should look.

There is a large lake in the grounds and a pretty walled garden, as well as the famous clipped yews, which stand like Easter Island statues – they are said to represent the multitude and the apostles.

Packwood was owned by the Featherstone family from the end of the 16th century until 1869 when Alfred Ash bought the house. Mr Ash's son Graham devoted his life to the Tudor recreation of the interior buying textiles and furnishings of the period from nearby house sales. It was he who gave the house to the National Trust in 1941. One of the most fascinating things about the house is that it has at least six sundials – but no one knows why!

BELOW: Packwood House is a stange mixture of both genuine and fake Elizabethan style.

SECRETS

PACKWOOD HOUSE, Packwood Lane, Lapworth, Warwickshire B94 6AT (nationaltrust.org.uk). ☎ 01564 782024. Open: Feb–Oct Tues–Sat 11.00–17.00. Price: House and grounds: adult £8.30, child £5.05.

While you're there

Visit the National Trust's Birmingham **BACK TO BACKS**. Victorian workers' cottages.

Secret place to stay

MALLORY COURT, Royal Leamington Spa (mallory.co.uk). A splendid manor house with luxury accommodation.

Bournville

WEST MIDLANDS

The Quakers' long history of practical good works and benevolence is best seen in the setting of this Birmingham suburb. It was in 1879 that the Cadbury brothers, George and Richard, took over the running of their father's chocolate factory. Their workers were revered and well paid in stark contrast to the conditions for most of the working classes. At their own expense the brothers developed Bournville, a remarkable model village, in which the architect was commissioned to design homes with the look and feel of old England, complete with village green but no public house. Two genuine medieval houses were dismantled and then reassembled in this Birmingham suburb.

Each well-built cottage in Bournville was provided with a bathroom – almost unheard of for working-class housing at the time – and the brothers made sure there was plenty of space for gardens and other green areas in

The model village of Bournville.

which to exercise, since the health of the workforce was paramount. The village became a model for other industrialists and the antidote to the cramped squalor in which much of the working classes lived.

Today the village is considered one of the nicest places to live, and the trust which runs the village continues.

SECRETS

While you're there

Visit the fascinating **BLACK COUNTRY MUSEUM**, which shows just what the heart of the industrial world looked like in the 19th century (bclm.co.uk).

Secret Place to stay

THE OLD TOWN HALL, Bewdley (bewdley-oldtownhall-bandb.co.uk). Late medieval building with homely feel.

Soho House

WEST MIDLANDS

Classical Soho House, in Handsworth, just 5km (3 miles) north of Birmingham was the the home of Matthew Boulton (1728–1809), a key figure in the industrial development of that city, and a friend of the scientist and engineer James Watt (1736–1819). The house, once considered a cottage, and situated next to Boulton's now demolished Soho Manufactory has been carefully restored to reflect the style of 18th-century Birmingham. As you walk through the splendid rooms it is easy to imagine Watt and Boulton discussing the developments that made Birmingham one of the great manufacturing centres of the world. The house was the setting for meetings of the Lunar Society, whose members included the leading figures of the day.

Matthew Boulton inherited his father's button-making business, and went on to produce objects in silver and gilded bronze in his Soho factory. His friendship with Watt led to the design and manufacture of steam engines that were eventually exported all over the world. Boulton's other great claim to fame is that he set up the world's first steam-powered mint at Soho.

Although, the city of Birmingham has encroached, Soho House provides a rare chance to see into the private life of one of the fathers of the Industrial Revolution.

One of Soho House's elegant rooms.

SECRETS

SOHO HOUSE, Soho Avenue, Handsworth, Birmingham, B18 5LB (bmag.org.uk/soho-house). ☎ 0121 554 9122. Open: Apr–Oct Tues–Sun & BH Mon 12.00–16.00. Price: adult £4, child free.

While you're there

BLAKESLEY HALL, Birmingham (www.bmag.org.uk/blakesley-hall). This beautiful timber-framed merchant's house was built in 1590 and lies hidden behind endless streets of suburban houses. ☎ 0121 464 2193.

Where to stay

THE OLD FARM HOTEL, Birmingham (oldfarmhotel.co.uk). Enjoys a great setting – minutes from the centre of Birmingham, yet within the historical village of Bournville and only a few miles from Soho House.

Clent Hills

WORCESTERSHIRE

This beautiful landscape deserves to be as well known as the South Downs or the Peak District – at roughly 300m (1,000ft) the summit offers wonderful views in all directions: across the Worcestershire Plain and Severn Valley towards Wales in the west, and over the Midlands, the Black Country and Birmingham in the east. At the top there is a group of four standing stones – but don't be fooled: the stones may look like a Neolithic or Bronze Age monument but they are not. They were placed here in the 18th century as a kind of folly, a self-conscious attempt at antiquarianism!

The Clent Hills are made up of three sandstone ridges with pollarded beeches and small groups of Scots pine planted here and there. There is also an arboretum and remnants of the original heathland landscape. Among the rare plants that grow in quiet undisturbed corners are bird's foot trefoil and cuckoo-flower.

Clent Hills offer good rambling country.

Brockhampton

WORCESTERSHIRE

Brockhampton is everything an ancient, small timber-framed English manor house should be – quaint, crooked, mellow and moated. Huge red-brick chimneys, positioned at each end of the house, seem almost to hold the it up. Brockhampton is L-shaped, with the great hall that would have been the place for entertainment open to the rafters, in the manner of the Saxon halls that would have been common all over England before the Norman Conquest.

The two-storey gatehouse, which is equally evocative, provides access over the moat to the house. With its upper storey jutting precariously out from the lower, it looks as if it is about to topple over. As this was a dangerous, lawless part of the Welsh Marches when the house was built (probably completed just before 1400), the moat was a genuine defensive feature, as well as a status symbol. A ruined chapel adds to the idyllic old England image.

The manor is surrounded by parkland filled with wildlife and ancient oak and beech trees. Apart from deer, the wooded landscape provides the opportunity to see a wide diversity of wildlife, from soaring buzzards to tiny dormice.

John Domulton, who built the house, was a descendant of the Brockhampton family, who had lived in this isolated valley since at least the early 12th century. The house stayed in the family until the line died out in the middle of the 20th century, at which point it was handed over to the National Trust. Latterly the house was used as a farmhouse.

Lovely Brockhampton manor house.

SECRETS

BROCKHAMPTON ESTATE
On the Herefordshire/Worcestershire border, 3km (2 miles) east of Bromyard (nationaltrust.org.uk). ☎ 01885 482077. Open: House Feb 11.00–16.30; Mar–Nov 11.00–17.00; Nov–Dec Sat, Sun 11.00–16.00. Price: adult £5.81, child £2.90, family £14.31.

While you're there

Visit nearby **HEREFORD** with its lovely unspoilt cathedral and ancient narrow streets and houses.

Secret place to stay

BRANDON LODGE, Hereford (brandonlodge.co.uk/). An attractive lodge with plenty of space situated just 1 mile from the city centre.

ENGLAND

North

FROM THE WILD moors of Northumberland to the splendours of the Yorkshire Dales and the Lake District, the North has as much to offer the visitor as anywhere in the world. And, tucked away in its wonderful landscape are numerous architectural and cultural gems. You can see George Stephenson's tiny cottage on the Tyne at Wylam, the outstanding gardens at Allen Banks, or the ancient watermill at Eskdale in Cumbria. Visit the little-known Duddon Valley, and in Wordsworth's hometown of Cockermouth, take in the fascinating museum of printing. In Lancashire discover spectacular Heysham Head, and in Yorkshire don't miss the remarkable village of Saltaire.

Eskdale Mill CUMBRIA

Eskdale is one of the loveliest valleys in Cumbria, and at its head is one of the last remaining corn mills in the north of England. Still complete with its original timber workings, the mill dates back to 1878.

Remarkably, the mill was still grinding corn until well into the 20th century. Much of the gearing was kept when a dynamo was installed, and the waterwheel continued to be used – right up to the mid 1950s – to generate electricity. The mill then lay quiet until the 1970s, when its importance was recognized, and it was bought by the local council and fully restored.

A permanent exhibition explains the history of the mill and how it works, but visitors can also see the mill regularly grinding corn, just as it has done for centuries.

SECRETS

ESKDALE WATERMILL (eskdalemill.co.uk). Open: Apr–Sep 11.30–17.30 (may be closed Mon, Sat). ☎ 01946 723335 to confirm opening times.

While you're there

Take a walk in the beautiful **ESKDALE VALLEY**, and you can reach the mill just as it would have been reached in earlier times – via an ancient packhorse bridge over the Whillan Beck in the splendidly named village of Boot.

Secret place to stay

BOOT INN, Eskdale (bootinn.co.uk). Small, unpretentious and good value.

Milling has been carried out at this site since a few years after the great Domesday survey.

The Printing House Museum CUMBRIA

Cockermouth is probably best known as the birthplace of the great romantic poet William Wordsworth, or more recently as the town that suffered the worst effects of the British weather when in 2009 the rivers Cocker and Derwent, which converge on the town, burst their banks during freak weather, causing destruction and loss and effectively cutting the town into two as the bridge that joined the two halves was swept away.

More positively, this little Cumbrian town is now home to a remarkable museum of printing. The museum – which is exceptionally well planned and laid out – takes the visitor through the history of printing from its invention in Europe, by Gutenberg, in the 15th century. The development of the printing press was revolutionary in its time, ultimately transforming the lives of ordinary people and providing access to the written word in a way that had never existed before. For the first time in history, books could be produced on a large scale, as movable type speeded up the process, which had previously been a laborious hand-crafted process.

Every innovation in the world of printing is included in this display, up until the 20th century – each revolutionary in its day. Visitors get the chance to try their hand at typesetting – not as easy as it looks! When you've set your page you can have it printed – or proofed, to use printers' jargon – on a hand press and take it home as a keepsake.

SECRETS

THE PRINTING HOUSE MUSEUM
102 Main Street, Cockermouth,
Cumbria, CA13 9LX ☎ 01900 824984.

While you're there

WORDSWORTH HOUSE, Cockermouth
(wordsworthhouse.org.uk).
Visit Wordsworth's modest birthplace and childhood home, which is vividly brought to life by costumed guides.

Secret place to stay

THE OLD POSTING HOUSE, Cockermouth
(oldpostinghouse.co.uk). It's 500 years old and with just four rooms, good service is guaranteed. This B&B has great views across the fells.

Try your hand at typesetting.

Duddon Valley

CUMBRIA

The Duddon River runs for just 27km (17 miles) from Wrynose Pass to the estuary at Broughton-in-Furness, but what this little river valley lacks in length and size it more than makes up for in scenic quality. In short, the Duddon Valley, with its woodlands and fells and its tumbling mysterious stream, is one of Cumbria's hidden gems. There is just one village along the valley – the delightful hamlet of Ulpha – which may explain the slightly forgotten feel to the valley's wooded slopes.

Near where the river starts its life at Wrynose Pass there is the beautiful – and ancient – Birks packhorse bridge. From here you can look down into the dark waters that provide a home for numerous native brown trout. Tiny roads wind along the valley, sometimes hugging the river, sometimes meandering away from it, but wherever you are there is much to enjoy. Ulpha Pass and Hardknott Fell should not be missed high up where the river Duddon begins. When you reach the sea at Broughton-in-Furness you should not miss Swineside ancient stone circle.

The Duddon Valley is a mix of woodlands, fells and tumbling crystalline streams.

SECRETS

While you're there

Visit **RAVENGLASS** the Lake District's own steam railway (ravenglass-railway.co.uk).

Secret place to stay

OLD KINGS HEAD, Broughton-in-Furness
☎ 01229 716293. One of the oldest buildings in the Lakes – don't miss it.

Hall-i'-th'-Wood

LANCASHIRE

Just to the north-east of Bolton is one of Britain's most remarkable – yet perhaps least known – ancient timber-framed houses. Set in the township of Tongue (the word deriving probably from the Old Norse 'tangi' or Old English 'tang', meaning 'a narrow strip of land'), Hall-i'–th'-Wood was built from timber cut down in the long-vanished ancient oak woodland that once covered this whole area.

The house was built in the early part of the 16th century, probably completed in 1530, by a wealthy local landowner called Lawrence Brownlow, who chose a high, easily defended position above Eagley Brook. When first built the house would have been isolated and surrounded by woodlands that provided a home for many of the animals we still know today, but also for wild boar. The house was

Exuberant decoration on Hall–i'–th'–Wood.

extended at the end of the 16th century and then again in the 1640s.

By 1758 the hall was being rented by the family of a remarkable man called Samuel Crompton. As a child Crompton watched his mother spinning yarn in one of the upstairs rooms at the hall, and he began to experiment with new ways to increase the speed and efficiency of weaving. Before he was 30 Crompton had invented the mule – the first multiple-spindle machine able to produce top-quality yarn.

During the 19th century the house fell into disrepair until it was rescued and restored by Lord Leverhulme in 1900. It is now a fascinating museum after being beautifully restored in the early 1990s.

SECRETS

HALL I'-TH'-WOOD MUSEUM
Green Way, Off Crompton Way, Bolton, BL1 8UA ☎ 01204 332370.

While you're there

Visit **CUERDEN VALLEY PARK** with its 263ha (650 acres) of woods, lawns and flowerbeds. A rural lung close to urban Preston (cuerdenvalleypark.org.uk).

Secret place to stay

WOODHALL HOTEL AND SPA, Linton, ☎ 01937 587271. Lovely old building with lots of charm and a great swimming pool.

HALL-I'-TH'-WOOD • LANCASHIRE

169

Heysham Head

LANCASHIRE

Cliffs of red Triassic sandstone at the seaward end of this wonderful headland provide glorious views across Morecambe Bay and the Lake District beyond. Mostly heathland with some woodland, Heysham also has much of archaeological interest, including the remains of spectacular rock-cut graves and the ruined 8th-century St Patrick's Chapel (a scheduled ancient monument), which gets its name from the legend that St Patrick came ashore here when his ship was wrecked off the Lancashire coast.

In spring you'll see carpets of bluebells across the headland where the bracken and bramble, grassland and low shrub cover allow. The areas of woodland support oak and elm,

ash and – rather too plentiful for some – the ubiquitous sycamore. Heysham cliffs are also the only home in this part of the world of the sea spleenwort, a rare fern.

Rock-cut graves at Heysham Head.

SECRETS

While you're there

Visit **SIZERGH CASTLE**, an ancient family home, holding the national collection of ferns in its spectacular gardens. (nationaltrust.org.uk).

Secret place to stay

RIVERSIDE HOTEL, Kendal (riversidekendal.co.uk). A pretty 17th-century building and reasonable rates.

Barton Swing Aqueduct MANCHESTER

The Barton Swing Aqueduct was built in 1893 to carry the Bridgewater Canal across the Manchester Ship Canal. The original stone aqueduct was so low that only relatively small vessels could pass underneath it. The swing aqueduct, which replaced it, was designed to allow larger boats to proceed up the Manchester Ship Canal.

The new aqueduct has massive gates at each end to seal water inside it, effectively like a tank. It then turns on a pivot at the centre of the aqueduct, until it is at right angles to the Bridgewater Canal (which it normally carries), thus allowing the bigger boats – up to 20,000 tons – to pass by on each side of it along the Manchester Ship Canal. It is a remarkable feat considering that the aqueduct is more than 70m (230ft) long and holds more than 800 tons of water. And, when you

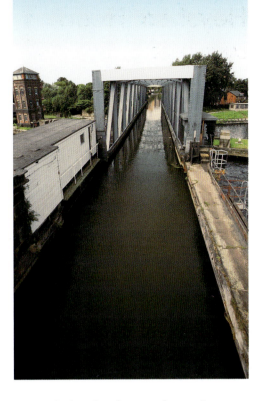

Barton Swing Aqueduct travels over the Manchester Ship Canal, and turns on a pivot so that ships can travel up the canal from the Mersey Estuary to the centre of Manchester.

add to that weight the additional weight of the aqueduct itself – another 800 tons – it is easy to see why the aqueduct is considered one of the wonders of the industrial world.

This extraordinary piece of engineering is testimony to the Victorian engineers' belief in progress; and their conviction that industry and effort could overcome any and every obstacle. Such was the faith in the design that the new aqueduct was built alongside the old one and could not be tested until the old one, itself a landmark, was demolished.

SECRETS

While you're there

Explore the **MANCHESTER SHIP CANAL** itself – one of the wonders of Britain's great industrial age.

Secret place to stay

PALACE HOTEL, Manchester (palace-hotel-manchester.co.uk). Manchester city centre has a wide variety of architectural styles. A few gems from Manchester's great industrial days do survive and you can stay in one in the centre of the city.

Beadnell Limekilns

NORTHUMBERLAND

If average temperatures in Northumberland were a little higher, the county's fabulous sandy beaches would be the talk of Europe. But the cold winds that slice in across the North Sea keep the beautiful, seemingly endless, stretches of sand uncluttered.

Among all the lovely villages of this windswept coast, Beadnell is one of the most interesting. The village's harbour walls and massive limekilns were built in the 18th century, and, despite being close to the main Great North Road that links Newcastle to Edinburgh, this is a quiet place with a slightly forgotten air. In earlier times, however, it was a bustling industrial centre: the massive kilns were fed daily with limestone mined from a big quarry to the south of the village, and when the lime had been burned it was loaded aboard ships and carried south to fertilize the fields of Lincolnshire, Kent, East Anglia and Sussex.

Beadnell was a lime-burning village – the limekilns were operated from the mid-1700s until 1858, and in that time the population of the village grew from a few dozen to more than 500. Before modern fertilizers, lime was a staple of agricultural success. The lime-burning process was relatively straightforward. First, fresh lime was poured into the top of the kiln with plenty of coal (five parts lime to one part coal) and the kiln was then fired to around 1000°C (1832°F) before being allowed to cool slowly. The valuable cooked lime was then removed from the base of the kiln.

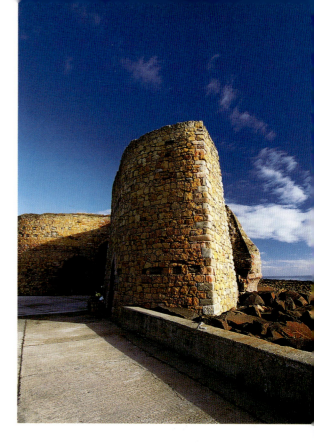

Old limekilns at Beadnell.

SECRETS

While you're there

Take a walk around **SEAHOUSES**, a pretty and often overlooked seaside village. It will give you a real sense of how Northumberland used to be.

Secret place to stay

CRASTER ARMS HOTEL, Beadnell (crasterarms.co.uk). An old building right in the middle of some of Northumberland's most spectacular coast.

Stephenson's Cottage

NORTHUMBERLAND

Stephenson's cottage, once the childhood home of George Stephenson (1781–1848) better known as the 'father of the railways', is a tiny isolated cottage on the banks of the river Tyne. Four families lived in this cottage, and Stephenson's humble family lived in just one room. Stephenson was illiterate until the age of 18, when he paid to learn to read and write. Yet he changed the world forever with his inventions. It was Stephenson's *Rocket* that launched the era of railway travel when, in September 1825, it ran from Darlington to Stockton carrying 450 people at a staggering 25km (15 miles) an hour.

SECRETS

GEORGE STEPHENSON'S BIRTHPLACE, Wylam, NE41 8BP (nationaltrust.org.uk). ☎ 01661 853457. Open: mid-Mar–Oct Thur–Sun 11.00–17.00. Price: adult £2, child £1.

While you're there

Visit nearby **CORBRIDGE** with its lovely old houses and medieval tower.

Secret place to stay

CRAG HOUSE HOTEL, Hexham (craghousebandb.co.uk/). ☎ 01434 681276. Beautifully situated on an alpaca farm.

The tiny stone-built cottage straddles the Tyne, about 19km (12 miles) inland from Newcastle and is open to the public to view.

George Stephenson's birthplace.

Bamburgh Castle

NORTHUMBERLAND

From the entrance to the internationally important bird sanctuary of Budle Bay, south to the great fortress castle of Bamburgh stretch the wide sands of one of Northumberland's best beaches. The walk between the two will take you little more than an hour, but it is worth it, for these beaches are never crowded and afford breathtaking views over wide, unspoiled vistas. Alternatively, you can walk south for many miles enjoying some of the most bracing sea airs and clean sands in Europe.

Bamburgh is a pretty sandstone village, famous as the birthplace of Victorian heroine Grace Darling (1815–42). One dreadful stormy night Grace, aged just 23, rowed out with her father to help save the crew of a boat wrecked on the Farne Islands. Overnight she became a national hero. She died young of consumption, but not before Queen Victoria had insisted on meeting her. A small museum – complete with replica rowing boat – commemorates her life.

Brooding over the village is the castle. Once a medieval fortress it was converted into more comfortable domestic accommodation in the 18th century, but set high on its rocky precipice it still seems to intimidate the humbler houses and cottages nestling below its walls.

Bamburgh Castle spans 3.6ha (9 acres) and is one of the largest inhabited castles in Britain.

SECRETS

BAMBURGH CASTLE (bamburghcastle.com). ☎ 01668 214515. Open: mid-Feb–Oct 10.00–17.00; Nov–mid-Feb Sat, Sun 11.00–16.30. Price: adult £9, child £4, family £22.

While you're there

Don't miss **LINDISFARNE ISLAND** just along the coast. Walk across the spectacular causeway at low tide and see where Christianity first came to Britain.

Secret place to stay

WHITE SWAN, Alnwick (classiclodges.co.uk/The_White_Swan_Hotel_Alnwick/). Set in the lovely town of Alnwick, home to the dukes of Northumberland for more than 1,000 years. You can also visit Alnwick Castle.

Allen Banks

NORTHUMBERLAND

Scenic views, a beautiful woodland garden, mature trees and an idyllic pond make up one of the north-east's best-kept secrets: Allen Banks. The gardens here were lovingly created by Susan Davidson between 1830 and 1860, using stone steps and paths to guide the visitor through a series of delightful vistas on the 81ha (200-acre) site on the banks of the Allen.

When you cross the suspension bridge that carries you across the steep ravine above the river, keep a lookout for dippers and wagtails, and then head south to Staward Wood, where there is a medieval tower house and gateway. Tower houses were once typical of this area, for Northumberland remained a lawless place until well into the 18th century. The border rievers (raiders) were continually feuding, organizing cattle raids and revenge attacks back and forth across the border with Scotland. The authorities could do little to police these remote uplands, which is why fortified houses remained the norm long after they had ceased to be built elsewhere in the country.

Staward Wood is said to be very ancient. Certainly it is rich in rare plants, including the wood fescue and moschatel, and it is one of the red squirrel's last English strongholds.

Suspension bridge over the river Allen.

SECRETS

ALLEN BANKS AND STAWARD GORGE
Bardon Mill, Hexham, Northumberland, NE47 7BU
(nationaltrust.org.uk).
Open all day every day.

While you're there

Don't miss one of the best sections of **HADRIAN'S WALL** and **HOUSESTEADS FORT**, which are close by.

Secret place to stay

LANGLEY CASTLE HOTEL, Hexham (langleycastle.com). One of the most romantic and beautifully set hotels in Northumberland.

Piece Hall

YORKSHIRE

Even as late as the 1970s, the Piece Hall, the last of England's great 18th-century cloth markets was in danger of demolition. Built in stone to a wonderful classical design – two storeys above an arched ground floor – and organized around a large cobbled square, the Piece Hall was once the centre of the commercial world for handloom weavers from villages and isolated cottages all over this part of Yorkshire. For the Piece Hall was where they sold their wares. It opened in 1779, but by the middle decades of the 19th century, handloom weaving had been all but obliterated by huge mechanized weaving mills. The Piece Hall struggled on and was even – in 1928 – officially recognized as an ancient monument. Of course the designation did nothing to secure its future, and on several occasions it nearly went the way of the cloth halls of Leeds, Bradford and Wakefield. All were demolished.

By the late 19th century the Hall was a wholesale market, and though it fell into disrepair the basic structure remained sound until restoration finally took place in 1972 – and what an extraordinary building it is. Today it is home to 300 wide-ranging independent shops and cafés, restaurants and other businesses.

Halifax's Piece Hall with its classical arcades is now a tourist attraction, but once dominated local industry.

SECRETS

PIECE HALL, Halifax
(thepiecehall.co.uk).

While you're there

BETTYS TEA ROOMS are legendary for their afternoon teas (bettys.co.uk), but you'll have to travel to York for the nearest café.

Secret place to stay

CROFT MILL, Hebden Bridge (croftmill.com). Luxury apartments in the heart of the spectacular Pennine Hills.

Saltaire

YORKSHIRE

Just to the north of Bradford and deep in Brontë country is the village of Saltaire. What makes Saltaire so special is that it was built to provide decent accommodation for factory workers at a time when most factory owners allowed their workers to live in conditions of the utmost poverty and degradation. The village was built as a 'model' or ideal village by the great woollen-mill owner Sit Titus Salt

ⓘ

SECRETS

While you're there

Visit the nearby **BRADFORD INDUSTRIAL MUSEUM**, which has a fascinating collection of international standing (bradfordmuseums.org/venues/industrialmuseum/).

The **NATIONAL MEDIA MUSEUM** holds the national collections of photography, cinematography, television and new media. The country's first IMAX threatre opened here.

Secret place to stay

OLD MANOR HOTEL, Bradford (oldmanorhotel.com). An attractive building and reasonable prices.

(1803–76), one of the most remarkable industrialists of that great period of industrial expansion that made Britain the commercial centre of the world.

Saltaire is such a remarkable place that, along with Stonehenge and Bath, it has been designated a World Heritage Site. The houses and shops are simple, brick-built and by no means grand, but compared to the Victorian slums of Manchester and Leeds, Saltaire must have seemed like heaven to industrial workers in the 19th century. The streets let in the light, the houses, with their generous-size windows, and are solid and well made. Unlike those pious mill and factory owners who went devoutly to church each Sunday, but worked their staff extraordinarily hard, Sir Titus Salt was both a businessman and a genuine, practical philanthropist. Saltaire is his monument.

The mills at Saltaire.

Bridestones Moor

YORKSHIRE

The heathland of Bridestones Moor.

The strange sandstone stacks that rise up from this lonely moor in the wilds of North Yorkshire were laid down as sediments at the bottom of the sea during the Jurassic period some 206 to 144 million years ago. Earth movements pushed them into their present position, and erosion over the countless millennia since has left them as the strange outcrops we see today. The stacks stare down at a rare heathland habitat of heather mixed with numerous sedges and other heathland plants, bilberry and crowberry among them.

Linked to Blakey Topping and Crosscliff, the moor is a Site of Special Scientific Interest looked after and managed by the National Trust. Many rare plants grow in cracks in the rocks here, including wall rue and maidenhair. At Dovedale Wood – one of the oldest areas of woodland in the country – there are ancient oaks mixed with thick luscious areas of fern and honeysuckle, moss and lichen. A 2.4km (1½-mile) nature trail runs through an excellent mix of these varied habitats.

Blakey Topping is one of the strangest parts of this remote and beautiful region – from the distance it rises up, cone shaped and heather clad, from a vast sea of green forest. The view from the top is one of the best-kept secrets of this part of Yorkshire.

SECRETS

While you're there

Visit the ruins of nearby **PICKERING CASTLE**, a splendid example of 13th- and 14th-century work (english-heritage.org.uk).

Secret place to stay

WHITE SWAN INN, Pickering (white-swan.co.uk). A charming old building, friendly staff and very reasonable prices. Pickering is an attractive town too, and well worth having a look around.

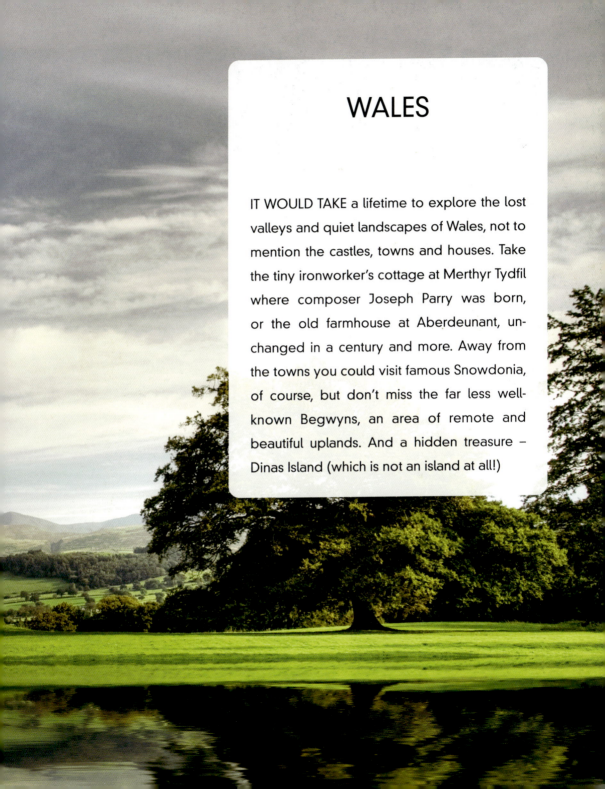

WALES

IT WOULD TAKE a lifetime to explore the lost valleys and quiet landscapes of Wales, not to mention the castles, towns and houses. Take the tiny ironworker's cottage at Merthyr Tydfil where composer Joseph Parry was born, or the old farmhouse at Aberdeunant, un-changed in a century and more. Away from the towns you could visit famous Snowdonia, of course, but don't miss the far less well-known Begwyns, an area of remote and beautiful uplands. And a hidden treasure – Dinas Island (which is not an island at all!)

Aberdeunant

CARMARTHENSHIRE

History comes alive when we see how people really lived in the past – not through court rolls and other official documents, but rather through the houses they lived in, the implements they used, the food they ate and the clothes they wore.

The old farmhouse at Aberdeunant brings history alive in this way because it is one of the few places in Wales where it is possible to see agricultural life as it really was before mechanization in the 20th century swept away 1,000 years of farming history. The house is delightful and rare partly

The farmland of Aberdeunant estate.

SECRETS

ABERDEUNANT, Taliaris, Llandeilo, Carmarthenshire, SA19 6DL (nationaltrust.org.uk) ☎ 01558 650177. Guided tour and appointment only April–Sep: first Sat and Sun of each month, 12.00–17.00.

While you're there

Don't miss the National Trust's **DOLAUCOTHI GOLD MINES**. They ceased working in 1938 but show evidence of gold-gathering back as far as Roman times. You can even have a go at panning for gold here.

Secret place to stay

PLOUGH INN, Llandeilo (ploughrhosmaen.com). A perfect base from which to explore the beautiful Tywi Valley.

because it is so tiny – only the *gegin fawr* (the farm kitchen) is open to the public.

The house is cruck-framed and may well have started life as a simple hall, a style of building that would have been familiar in Saxon times.

Out in the farmyard, evidence of the way in which this remote farm developed over the centuries is clear – the barn, tool shed and stable date variously from the late 17th through to the 19th centuries. Built of local stone they are slate-roofed, although the farmhouse itself still has its thatch.

One of the most remarkable things about Aberdeunant is that the land around it has never been intensively farmed. Its pastures and meadows have never been 'improved', sprayed or ploughed according to modern methods, which is why, every spring and summer, they are gloriously rich in flora.

Aberglasney Gardens

CARMARTHENSHIRE

One of the country's best-kept secrets, this beautiful house has a mysterious past. Largely rebuilt early in the 18th century, its origins are said to lie in the early 15th century, though no one seems quite sure of this. The house sits quietly in the lovely Tywi valley. Unlike many ancestral homes that remain with one family for centuries, Aberglasney has changed hands at a regular pace. Each new custodian has brought hope and generous finances to the property only to leave it several generations later unable to continue the upkeep.

Today, the whole of one wing is open to the elements, and the house is gradually being restored, having been purchased by a trust to save the property and its gardens. The gardens are the real treasure at Aberglasney. The yew tunnel – a row of ancient yews carefully trained to grow over each other – is unique in Britain. The Courtyard Garden is also a remarkable survivor – one side is formed by the house, while the other three sides are supported on a series of stone arches. Almost every example of this type of raised-walkway courtyard garden vanished in the 18th century as the fashion for all things 'Capability Brown' swept through the British Isles, but Aberglasney, kept its old-style garden which was rediscovered under dense vegetation in the 1990s.

The Cloister Garden.

SECRETS

ABERGLASNEY GARDENS, Llangathen, Carmarthenshire, SA32 8QH (aberglasney.org). Open: Apr–Sep 10.00–14.00, Oct–Mar 10:30–16.00. Price: adult £6.36, child £3.63.

While you're there
Make sure you explore the lovely **TYWI VALLEY**. Of particular interest are the remains of Grongaer, an Iron Age hill fort.

Secret place to stay
CAWDOR HOTEL, Llandeilo (thecawdor.com). A listed Georgian building.

Conwy

CONWY

Conwy is a remarkably well-preserved medieval town still with its encircling walls. Centuries after they were first built, the medieval walls, which in places are 8m (26ft) thick, still have their forts, each precisely 45m (150yd) from the last, and each a stronghold in its own right. Conwy would have been an impregnable town when Edward I (1239–1307) established his castle here. It was one of a series of castles that marked the border at that time between the Welsh and the English.

There are 21 bastions, and visitors can walk right around the town on the wall, which rises quickly from the West Gate until it reaches its highest point at the north-west corner tower. From here you can look out across the estuary, or back across a town that looks much as medieval London might have done. Luckily for Conwy, all 1,283m (1,400yd) of the old walls

Conwy Castle within the town walls.

were allowed to remain, along with many of the old houses within the walls – somehow the town planners and architects of the 1960s and 1970s were kept at bay.

Conwy Castle, a dark forbidding sight even today, sits high above the town, but within the town walls, on a knoll. The castle was built in the late 13th century by a mason brought in specially by the king from mainland Europe.

Portmeirion

GWYNEDD

Bright, quirky, charming, eccentric and delightful – over the years these and many similar words have been used to describe this highly stylized village on the Welsh coast. It would take an architectural historian to explain every style or parody of style contained in this village, which is essentially the life's work of one man – the architect Clough Williams-Ellis (1883–1978).

In many ways Williams-Ellis was a man ahead of his time. He wanted to prove that building did not necessarily ruin a beautiful place, which is why he spent nearly 50 years (1925–75) building this village on the peninsula that he owned. With its whitewashed or pastel-coloured cottages, Portmeirion looks like something from the Mediterranean, but it does just what its architect intended it to do – it fits well into an area of outstanding natural beauty, surrounded as it is by gardens and woodlands and miles of beautiful beach. Williams-Ellis was a passionate conservationist long before such notions were fashionable, and he would be delighted to know that, today, the village to which he devoted his life is in the hands of a trust – a registered charity called The Second Portmeirion Foundation, which carefully guards his legacy.

The Portmeirion Hotel lets all the cottages in the village and there are restaurants, shops and delightful walks. But perhaps Portmeirion's greatest claim to fame is that it was the setting for the cult 1960s TV series *The Prisoner*.

It's hard to believe that this is a Welsh town.

SECRETS

While you're there

Just enjoy the spectacular **COASTAL WALKS** in this lovely region.

Secret place to stay

PORTMEIRION HOTEL, Portmeiron (portmeirion-village.com). Right in the heart of the village and remarkably unchanged since 1926.

Newborough Beach ISLE OF ANGLESEY

Just 3km (2 miles) south of the village of Newborough, a stone's throw from the road, is a hidden beach of quite breathtaking beauty. Newborough Beach is one of the most spectacular places along this weather-worn Atlantic coast. Mile after mile of pure white sand make the hustle and bustle of life seem an age away. There are superb views to distant Snowdonia and the Lleyn Peninsular and, if you turn left after reaching the beach from the car park, an hour's walking will bring you to the spectacular Menai Straits. Retrace your steps and turn right and the wide sands will bring you to Llanddwyn Island, a narrow strip of land cut off now and again by high tides.

From the car park to the Menai Straits, the sand dunes here – known as Newborough Warren – are a rich and varied nature reserve.

The white sands of Newborough Beach.

Among the species that come here to breed are Canada geese, teal and shelduck. Summer visitors include oystercatcher, ringed plover and lapwing and there healthy populations of kestrels and sparrowhawks. Behind the dunes the pine forest is rich in birdlife – including crossbills – and there are numerous footpaths through this remote and lovely mixture of freshwater lake, mudflat and tidal inlet.

Joseph Parry's Cottage MERTHYR TYDFIL

This small, unassuming house makes no claims to greatness. It is a typical ironworker's house from the 1840s, and its survival can be attributed to the fact that Dr Joseph Parry, arguably the best-known composer from Wales, was born here in 1841.

Parry moved to America with his family when he was just 13, but his prodigious talents were recognized and money was raised to return him to England to study at the Royal Academy of Music. He was a prolific composer whose work includes operas, songs

Composer Joseph Parry's birthplace.

and pieces for piano, but today he is best known for his hymns 'Aberystwyth' and 'Myfanwy'. In later life he became Professor of Music at the University College of Wales, before establishing his own private college, and then moving to tutor at Cardiff University.

Today the cottage where he was born looks just as it would have looked when Parry was a boy – furniture and decoration from the period combine with memorials of Dr Parry to create a unique glimpse of life in Merthyr Tydfil more than a century and a half ago.

SECRETS

JOSEPH PARRY'S COTTAGE 4 Chapel Row, Georgetown, Merthyr Tydfil, CF48 1BN
☎ 01685 727371. Open: Apr–Sep
Thurs–Sun 14.00–17.00.

While you're there

Visit **BIG PIT**, the national coal mine and museum where you can still descend almost 100m (328ft) to the coal face – a journey underground that faced hundreds of miners every day of their working lives over the centuries when coal was the lifeblood of this area
(museumwales.ac.uk/en/bigpit/).

Secret place to stay

ANGEL HOTEL, Abergavenny
(angelabergavenny.com).
Offers comfort and good food. The hotel recently won an award for its afternoon tea.

The Kymin

MONMOUTHSHIRE

The Wye Valley is not seen as a major tourist attraction, which is surprising given how unspoilt it is – so many places deserve mention that it is difficult to single them out, with one exception: the Kymin. High above the town of Monmouth, this beautiful wooded garden hides the Round House. Built as a place for banquets towards the end of the 18th century, the Round House provided a venue for the gentlemen of Monmouth to hold regular Tuesday lunches. Originally the lunches were held in the open air, but a year after they began in 1794, a heavy downpour persuaded the gentlemen to build the house we see today. For a shilling and sixpence the Round House dining room could be hired, and from its five windows guests could look out across 10 counties (weather permitting).

Such was the popularity of the Round House that the gardens were landscaped, walks and seats were built, a bowling green installed and a telescope provided on the roof 'for the pleasure of the more scientific among us'. The National Trust has restored the Round House, which now looks much as it did when the gentlemen of Monmouth first came to dine here more than two centuries ago.

Close to the Round House is a monument to Admiral Lord Nelson (and other admirals of the Fleet). It was built in 1801 and Nelson actually came here to see it soon after it was built.

The entrance to the Round House is secluded.

ⓘ

SECRETS

THE KYMIN
Overlooking Monmouth in the Wye Valley area of outstanding natural beauty on Offa's Dyke footpath (nationaltrust.org.uk). Open: Mar–Oct Mon, Sat, Sun 11.00–16.00.

While you're there

Visit the WEIR, a stunning riverside garden with sweeping views along the river Wye and the Herefordshire countryside (nationaltrust.org.uk).

Secret place to stay

RIVERSIDE HOTEL, Monmouth (riversidehotelmonmouth.co.uk). A small, friendly, family-run hotel in the heart of nearby Monmouth.

St Govan's Chapel

PEMBROKESHIRE

Hidden away on the wild remote Pembrokeshire coast is St Govan's Chapel, a minuscule stone-built cell built in the 13th century that seems almost to cling to a sheer cliff face. It is difficult to imagine a more austere, unworldly spot.

No one quite knows who St Govan was – he is not recorded in any early texts – but there is a theory that he may have been the Sir Gawain of Arthurian legend. According to one legend, St Govan or Gawain was pursued to this lonely rock face by invading Vikings, and it was only the intervention of the Holy Spirit (or some such supernatural agency) that allowed the rock to open just enough to let St Govan in but keep his pursuers out. Curious markings on the wall at the back of the chapel are said to show where St Govan's ribs brushed the wall as the rock opened to receive him, but whatever the truth or otherwise of the legends the chapel is a remarkable place.

Archaeological evidence suggests it may replace a 6th century, or earlier, building. To reach it you have to use the steep steps cut into the cliff face itself, but the journey is well worth it if only for the spectacular views out across the sea. You might wonder what drove the early Christians to reject the world as it was and spend their lives in an isolated spot such as this.

St Govan's Chapel blends into the rocks.

SECRETS

While you're there

Visit the gorgeous **BEACH** at nearby Broad Haven South.

Secret place to stay

WOLFSCASTLE HOTEL, Haverfordwest (wolfscastle.com). Spectacularly situated.

Dinas Island

PEMBROKESHIRE

It's easy to see why the early Christians came to the Pembrokeshire coast – even today it is one of those rare places where it is possible to feel a real sense of escape from the pressures of the world. Dinas Island with its 40ha (100 acres) of heath and bracken-covered grazing land, is one of the less well-known treasures along the coast. In fact, it isn't an island at all; it's a headland separated from the mainland by a deep, narrow channel that was cut by a glacier, and which was then slowly filled with layers of peat over thousands of years.

Today numerous paths and a circular walk allow the visitor to explore the spectacular headland with its wonderful views across Cardigan Bay. At Pen Castell archaeologists believe there are the remains of an Iron Age hill fort, but the real pleasure of Dinas – apart from the views – is the fact that it is little visited and that it is home to important colonies of guillemot, fulmar and razorbill. On the seaward-facing, bracken-covered slopes there are also colonies of small blue butterfly and thrift clearwing moth.

Dinas Island (actually a headland) provides wonderful sea views on a clear day.

SECRETS

While you're there

Why not walk a section of the long-distance **PEMBROKESHIRE PATH?**

Secret place to stay

MANOR TOWN HOUSE, Fishguard (manortownhouse.com). This Georgian guest house in the heart of Fishguard is well worth a visit.

SECRETS

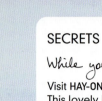

While you're there

Visit **HAY-ON-WYE** just a few miles away.
This lovely historic town has the largest
number of second-hand bookshops of
any town in Britain!

Secret place to stay

THE OLD BLACK LION, Hay-on-Wye
(oldblacklion.co.uk).
A fascinating building whose origins lie in
the 1300s. Perfect if you'd also like to
explore the nearby Brecon Beacons.

The Begwyns

POWYS

Snowdonia is probably the best-known area of countryside in Wales, but there are other places just as rare and special throughout the principality – one such is the Begwyns. Here on the extreme southern edge of the Radnorshire Commons there are unparalled views far out across the Brecon Beacons and the Black Mountains.

This remote and beautiful upland – nearly 527ha (1,300 acres) in all – runs along the ridge of the hills and is almost hemmed in by the wealth of valleys, towns and distant farms that surround it.

Comparatively little visited, the Begwyns are also important from an archaeological point of view. The whole of this upland common is a mass of ancient boundaries and enclosures. Habitation seems to have been particularly dense in earlier times at the southern tip of the plateau; archaeologists have discovered the remains of dozens of long-vanished houses, tracks and field boundaries here, evidence almost certainly of an abandoned medieval village.

But apart from splendid views and rich archaeology, the Begwyns are worth visiting for their wonderful birdlife – on any day in summer visitors can look up and there is a good chance they will see curlews, or buzzards drifting lazily across the sky, or hovering so high up as to be almost invisible, the skylark.

Usually free of visitors the Begwyns offer wonderful walking country.

SCOTLAND

FROM ORKNEY SITUATED off the far north coast of Scotland to the lowlands of Dumfries and Galloway, Scotland's unique landscapes and rich culture provide an unrivalled experience for the visitor. A good starting point is the fascinating 18th-century industrial village of New Lanark, or the unspoilt area of Culross on the Firth of Forth. On Islay you can visit the splendid distillery at Bowmore where whisky is made much as it was in the 1700s. And, if you fancy the really bizarre, yet beautiful, visit the Dunmore Pineapple near Stirling.

Bowmore Distillery

ARGYLL & BUTE

Scotland has many distilleries – hardly surprising when one remembers that whisky has made Scotland famous throughout the world – but one of the earliest and least modernized is on the island of Islay.

Bowmore was built on the shores of Loch Indaal in 1779. It's had just five owners in more than two centuries, and each has continued to produce whisky using techniques identical to those used in the earliest days.

Oak casks destined for Bowmore's fine whisky.

SECRETS

BOWMORE DISTILLERY
(bowmore.com/our-home/distillery/the-distillers).

While you're there

Go to **ISLAY HOUSE SQUARE** in Bridgend. From here it is a short walk to the famous **BRIDGEND WOODLANDS** and their fabulous display of woodland flowers.

Secret place to stay

BOWMORE HOTEL, Bowmore (bowmorehotel.co.uk).
Excellent cooking using local produce, and an attractive old house.

With each passing year, fewer distilleries are able to continue these ancient traditions – Bowmore for example, still employs a maltman. His job is to turn the barley on what is known as the malting floor using a specially designed wooden shovel.

But, of course, the heart of every good whisky is the water from which it is made – Bowmore whisky gets its water from the Laggan River. To reach the peaty river the water has first spent 2,000 years slowly percolating through the rocky hills above, and it is this – the precise nature of the rocks, the richness of the peat and the presence of Bowmore at the sea's edge – that enables the distillery to produce a whisky that is highly sought after by connoisseurs all over the world.

Perhaps the most interesting part of the distillery is the vaults – ancient, damp and pretty much unchanged since the distillery was first built – they are filled with giant oak barrels where the whisky is allowed to mature for decades before it is ready for sale.

Crossraguel Abbey AYRSHIRE

A surprising amount of Crossraguel Abbey still survives, despite the destruction caused by the Reformation and the later plundering for building materials. The abbey's gatehouse, with its curious corner turret, still survives almost intact and visitors can climb the stairs to enjoy the fine view out over the abbey grounds and the countryside beyond.

The abbey was a Cluniac foundation – a reformed Benedictine order that began at Cluny in France in about 900. The name Crossraguel probably comes from the Gallic for 'Cross of Riaghail'. Riaghail, or St Regulus, was a Greek monk who landed in Scotland in the Dark Ages.

The unusual corner tower of Crossraguel Abbey.

Over the centuries the buildings were extended, but then in 1560 came destruction. Unlike so many abbeys that were razed to the ground, Crossraguel, perhaps because of its isolated position, survived, or at least much of its built fabric did.

Today, the 15th-century choir building, with its beautiful carvings still in place, is open to the public, along with the gatehouse, and wherever you look from the top of the gatehouse tower the glorious Ayrshire countryside stretches away into the distance.

SECRETS

CROSSRAGUEL ABBEY
(historic-scotland.gov.uk). ☎ 01655 883113.
Open: Apr–Sep 9.30–17.30.
Price: adult £4, child £2.40.

While you're there

Just enjoy the **COUNTRYSIDE** round about – there are footpaths aplenty. And the small town of Maybole, ancient capital of Carrick, is just a few miles away and well worth exploring. The main street has many fine buildings, which provide character to the area.

Secret place to stay

ONE BARGANOCK, Maybole
(onebarganock.co.uk).
Luxurious and spacious.

Inchcolm Island

FIFE

A short journey out across the Firth of Forth, over the intriguingly named stretch of water known as Mortimer's Deep, will take you to one of the least-known of Scotland's many islands. In early medieval times the bleak, windswept island was the sole preserve of perhaps just two or three monks linked to St Columba (*c*.521–97), an Irish priest descended from the great kings of Ireland who is said to have brought Christianity to Scotland. The monks' tiny stone hut can still be seen.

In 1123 a great storm forced King Alexander I to take shelter on Inchcolm. He was so well looked after by the monks during his time on the island that he decided to build the monastery and the remains can still be seen today – or at least that's the legend. We know that an Augustinian abbey was established here by 1223 and its remains are among the best monastic ruins in Scotland. Today, they are the haunt of gulls and other seabirds, for the island is now uninhabited, but it is a beautiful place to visit and well worth the trip out from either Aberdour or South Queensferry.

The best-preserved group of monastic buildings in Scotland.

SECRETS

INCHCOLM ABBEY
(historic-scotland.gov.uk) ☎ 01383 823332.
Open: Apr–Sep 9.30–17.30; Oct 9.30–16.30.
Price: adult £5, child £3.

While you are there

Visit **ABERDOUR** just across the water. It is
enjoyable just to walk the quiet streets and
gaze at the fine stone buildings or the
silver sands of the town beach.

Secret place to stay

ABERDOUR HOTEL, Aberdour
(aberdourhotel.co.uk).
In the heart of the old town.

Culross

FIFE

Most of us probably associate the idea of 'pretty' villages with the gentle settlements of the south of England rather than the more rugged Scottish uplands, but hidden away here and there Scotland has many beautiful villages that are a delight to visit. Perhaps the most beautiful of all is Culross.

Remotely situated on the Firth of Forth this perfect little settlement is the least spoilt example of a late 17th-century burgh town. Carefully restored and limewashed, the houses are architecturally typical of Scotland at that time: most have crows'-feet gables, pantile roofs and deeply set windows. The narrow cobbled streets around which the houses seem almost to huddle are just as they would have been when wealthy merchants walked these streets 300 years ago at a time when Culross was Scotland's wealthiest town.

The National Trust for Scotland owns many of the houses, including the splendid 'palace' (which isn't a palace at all!). This was built for the 17th-century industrialist Sir George Bruce, and it still has its pleasing painted wooden ceilings. The study, which was built in 1600, has a tower that would have allowed the original owners to look out across the sea for incoming ships: vitally important since the town's prosperity was built on moving goods by sea. Other houses almost certainly date back to the 1600s, and one has the date 1577 on its gable, along with a brass plaque that proclaims: 'In this spot in 1832 nothing happened!'

Culross Abbey towers above the village.

SECRETS

While you're there

Climb up to **CULROSS ABBEY** (historic-scotland.gov.uk). The present church is made up of the eastern part of the old abbey. The rest of the abbey lies in ruins round about.

Secret place to stay

BONSYDE HOUSE HOTEL, Linlithgow (bonsydehouse.co.uk). Comfortable rooms and great food.

New Lanark

LANARKSHIRE

Despite its designation as a World Heritage Site, New Lanark – a complete industrial village dating back to the 18th century – is not as often visited as it could be. New Lanark was a workers' village – a settlement that was purpose-built to provide houses for those who worked in the cotton mill.

What makes New Lanark unique is that it is a monument to a remarkable man. That man was Robert Owen (1771–1858), whose philosophies and treatment of his workers were, at least, a century ahead of their time. Most mill owners and managers of the time allowed their workers to live in utmost poverty, with dreadful sanitation, no health care, the poorest-quality food, and working for 16 hours per day. Owen, on the other hand, built good quality housing, which still stands today in New Lanark. He set up schools for the mill workers' children, organized evening classes for adult workers, provided free health care and made available affordable food for all. Most remarkable of all, he refused to allow young children to work in the factory, providing them instead with a decent education. He also banned all corporal punishment.

Owen was mill manager at New Lanark from 1800 to 1825 – and there is no doubt that he would be delighted to see how his village has been preserved and restored. An award-winning visitor centre explains the importance of New Lanark and the legacy of Robert Owen.

Robert Owen's remarkable village for workers.

SECRETS

NEW LANARK VISITOR CENTRE, New Lanark Mills, Lanark. ML11 9DB (newlanark.org/). Open: Apr–Sep 10.00–17.00; Oct–Mar 11.00–17.00. Price: adult £8.50, child £6.

While you're there

Just a mile away are the **FALLS OF CLYDE**, a lovely riverside walk through trees filled with wildlife.

Secret place to stay

OLD MILL HOTEL, Motherwell (theoldmillhotelmotherwell. co.uk). On the banks of the river Calder.

Tugnet Ice House

MORAY

If you would like to see the last remains of a once-flourishing Scottish industry, Tugnet is the place to do it. Here stands a great barrel-roofed Georgian ice house, looking out over the estuary of the Spey.

Before high-seas netting and over-fishing generally, Scottish salmon filled the east and west coast rivers each spring and summer – so much so that catching and selling these much-prized fish was once a sustainable industry that employed many local people.

The ice house can be visited free of charge and with its spectacular brick-arched ceilings it is a splendid sight – its size (it's the biggest ice house in Scotland) reveals just how many salmon were once taken each year from these windswept coastal waters. The fish were

Tugnet Ice House near the Spey estuary has six vaulted rooms.

packed in ice here before starting on the long journey south to London or beyond. Salmon are still brought here, but in far smaller numbers. Once scientists discovered where at sea the Atlantic salmon fed, commercial netting in Scotland's river estuaries was doomed – all the fish, or most of them, were taken by trawlers on the feeding grounds.

SECRETS

TUGNET ICE HOUSE
Spey Bay, Fochabers, Moray, IV32 7DU
☎ 01249 449500. Phone before visiting.

While you're there

Try the **SPEYSIDE LONG DISTANCE WALK**, or just part of it. It ends, or begins, at the Tugnet Ice House.

Secret place to stay

THE GORDON ARMS HOTEL, Fochabers (gordonarms.co.uk). A hotel that has been enchanting guests for more than two centuries.

Dounby Click Mill

ORKNEY

The island of Orkney is incredibly rich in prehistoric sites – from the remarkable stone-built tomb of Maeshowe to the 5,000-year-old village at Skara Brae, but less well known and of more recent date are the click mills. These mills were common across Orkney until relatively recent times. One of the best preserved – and the only one still in working order – is at Dounby. It was probably built early in the 19th or towards the end of the 18th century, and it reveals an ingenious and simple solution to the problem of harnessing power for grinding corn.

Not having any powerful rivers available, the islanders built low stone buildings above fast-flowing streams, and as the stream flowed through its natural channel under the building, it rushed over the horizontally placed paddles of a specially designed wheel. An axle from the centre of this wheel went up through the floor above and was fixed to the centre of a grindstone, which was turned by the force of the water. These mills were just one step up from grinding corn by hand, but they would produce enough corn for a few families.

And the curious name? It comes from the noise made by a peg on the upper millstone, designed to strike the grainspout to ensure a steady flow of grain into the hole in the centre of the stone.

Dounby's corn-grinding click mill.

SECRETS

MAESHOWE TOMB
(historic-scotland.gov.uk).
Open: Apr–Sep 9.30–17.30; Oct–Mar
9.30–16.30. Price: adult £5.50, child £3.30.
Book in advance at Torniston Mill Visitor
Centre ☎ 01856 761606.

While you're there

Don't miss the **RING OF BRODGAR** at
Stenness – a 4,000-year-old circle of ancient
stones. Unusually, the stones are carefully
placed to create an almost perfect circle.

Secret place to stay

ORKNEY HOTEL, Kirkwall
(orkneyhotel.co.uk).
Traditional with a modern touch.

Maeshowe Tomb

ORKNEY

Neolithic remains exist all over Britain, but it is extremely rare to find those that show precisely how these distant ancestors built with wood or stone. One place where their extraordinary skills as stonemasons is evident is at Maeshowe in Orkney.

A 16m (52ft)-long, square, stone-lined passageway – precisely aligned with the position of the winter solstice – leads into the tomb where the real skills of those 5,000-year-old stonemasons become apparent. At first it is difficult to believe that such precise architecture could be the work of a people whom we think of as extremely primitive – surely the pre-literate hunter gatherers who came here could not have cut and fitted them in this precise way? Layers of slab stones cut precisely to fit rise gracefully to the corbelled ceiling, which is still complete. Small stones have been shaped to fit awkward places and throughout there is a strong sense of coherent planning.

When you leave Maeshowe it is easy to believe that you are still in the centre of a most important Neolithic area, for just 10 minutes' walk away are the four ancient stones of Stenness. The tallest of these standing stones rises 5m (17ft) and their shadows almost lie across the prehistoric village of Barnhouse, where some of the houses still have their internal features, including a stone fireplace carefully fixed in the centre of the floor.

The tomb is encircled by a bank and ditch.

Wade's Bridge

PERTH & KINROSS

This was the first bridge built across Scotland's longest river, the Tay, and helped complete a network of roads built by General George Wade (1673–1748) on behalf of the English crown. Wade's network of roads were designed to destroy the power of the lawless clans by providing easy access for English forces to enter Scotland and subdue any disturbance or discontent among the Highland Scots – rebellions such as the Jacobite rising of 1715. Wade's work in Scotland took a total of nine years, and in that time he oversaw the construction of more than 400km (250 miles) of road and dozens of smaller bridges.

His bridge at Aberfeldy – beautifully made in grey chlorite schist from a local quarry – was so well made that it is still open to traffic today. The bridge has five arches and is nearly 122m (400ft) long – a triumph of elegant 18th-century engineering in what was then a very remote region. William Adam, the

Wade's Bridge at Aberfeldy.

greatest Scottish architect of the day, was employed to design the bridge and it took an average of 400 men nearly a year to complete. The total cost was £3,596, which is the equivalent of more than £1 million today.

Bonnie Prince Charlie, pretender to the British throne used this extraordinary bridge in 1746 as he retreated north on his way toward defeat at Culloden.

Wade's other great claim to fame is that he used most of the stone from what was still a very well-preserved Hadrian's Wall to provide rubble and hard core for his road across from Newcastle to Carlisle.

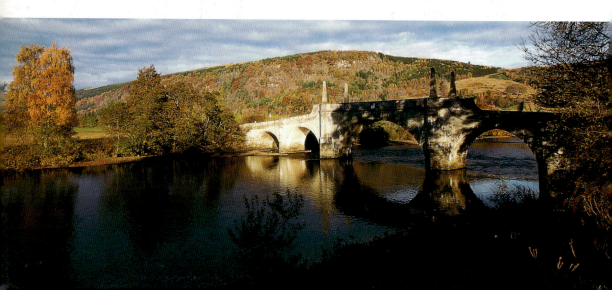

Dunmore Pineapple

STIRLINGSHIRE

Just a few miles south of Stirling is one of Scotland's most bizarre buildings – the Dunmore Pineapple. Built in 1761 at a time when pineapples and other exotic fruit were still rare and extremely costly, the 14m (46ft-) high sandstone pineapple is actually a sort of gazebo – a place where the Laird of Dunmore could look out across his gardens and land.

The pineapple is part of a walled garden and reflects the fact that pineapples were being grown in that garden in the 18th century – being able to grow such exotic fruit at that time was a huge status symbol and the stone pineapple would have announced that fact to the world. The Dunmore gardens, the

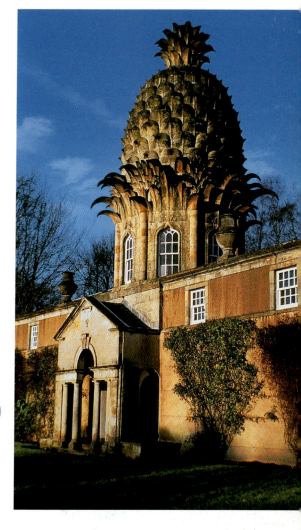

The Dunmore Pineapple is a folly par excellence.

Pineapple and 6.5ha (16 acres) of surrounding land – the policies, as the land is known in Scotland – were given to the Landmark Trust by the Countess of Perth in 1974. They are now a rich haven for plants and wildlife, including the rare great-crested newt.

ⓘ SECRETS

If you are really taken with **THE PINEAPPLE**, you can stay in it by contacting: The Landmark Trust, Shottesbrooke, Maidenhead, Berkshire, SL6 3SW (landmarktrust.org.uk). ☎ 01628 825925.

While you're there

Don't miss the well-signposted **WALK** through the unspoilt local woodlands.

Secret place to stay

AIRTH CASTLE, Airth (airthcastlehotel.com). Try staying in a real ancient castle.

This revised edition published in 2012 by
New Holland Publishers (UK) Ltd

First published in the UK in 2005 by
New Holland Publishers (UK) Ltd
London • Cape Town • Sydney • Auckland

www.newhollandpublishers.com

Garfield House, 86–88 Edgware Road,
London, W2 2EA, United Kingdom

80 McKenzie Street, Cape Town 8001, South Africa

Unit 1, 66 Gibbes Street, Chatswood,
NSW 2067, Australia

218 Lake Road, Northcote, Auckland, New Zealand

10 9 8 7 6 5 4 3 2 1

ISBN 978 1 84773 947 6

Publisher: Guy Hobbs
Editor: Sally MacEachern
Proofreader: Elspeth Anderson
Designer: Isobel Gillan
Cover designer: Rod Teasdale
Picture research: Susannah Jayes
Cartographer: Bill Smuts
Production: Marion Storz

Printed and bound in China by Toppan Leefung
Printing Ltd